Joomla! Template Design

Create your own professional-quality templates
with this fast, friendly guide

A complete guide for web designers to all aspects of
designing unique website templates for the free Joomla!
PHP Content Management System

Tessa Blakeley Silver

[PACKT] PUBLISHING

BIRMINGHAM - MUMBAI

Joomla! Template Design

Create your own professional-quality templates with this fast, friendly guide

First published: June 2007

Production Reference: 1190607

Published by Packt Publishing Ltd.
32 Lincoln Road
Olton
Birmingham, B27 6PA, UK.

ISBN 978-1-847191-44-1

www.packtpub.com

Cover Image by www.visionwt.com

Credits

Author

Tessa Blakeley Silver

Reviewer

Jayme Cousins

Senior Acquisition Editor

David Barnes

Development Editor

Mithil Kulkarni

Technical Editor

Saurabh Singh

Code Testing

Akshara Aware

Editorial Manager

Dipali Chittar

Project Manager

Patricia Weir

Project Coordinator

Sagara Naik

Indexer

Bhushan Pangaonkar

Proofreaders

Martin Brooks

Chris Smith

Production Coordinator

Shantanu Zagade

Cover Designer

Shantanu Zagade

About the Author

Tessa Blakeley Silver has her background in print design and traditional illustration. Over the years, she has evolved herself into the fields of web and multimedia development focusing on usability and interface design. Prior to starting her consulting and development company hyper3media (pronounced hyper-cube media) `http://hyper3media.com`, Tessa was the VP of Interactive Technologies at eHigherEducation, an online learning and technology company developing compelling multimedia simulations, interactions, and games that meet online educational requirements like 508, AICC, and SCORM. She has also worked as a consultant and freelancer for J. Walter Thompson and The Diamond Trading Company (formerly known as DeBeers). She was a Design Specialist and Senior Associate for PricewaterhouseCoopers' East Region Marketing department. Tessa authors several design and web technology blogs. *Joomla! Template Design* is her first book.

About the Reviewer

Jayme Cousins started creating commercial websites once released from University with a degree in Geography. His projects include marketing super-niche spatial analysis software, preparing online content overnight for his city's newspaper, printing road names on maps, painting houses, and teaching College tech courses to adults. He currently lives behind a keypad in London, Canada with his wife Heather and newborn son Alan. Jayme previously reviewed *Learning Mambo* from Packt Publishing. He enjoys matching technology with real-world applications for real-world people and often feels that his primary role is that of a translator of technobabble for entrepreneurs.

Jayme now provides web development, consulting, and technical training through his business, In House Logic (`www.inhouselogic.com`).

Table of Contents

Preface

Joomla! is a free, award-winning content management system written in PHP that allows users to easily publish their content on the World Wide Web and intranets.

The Joomla! template is a series of files within the Joomla! CMS that control the presentation of the content. The template is the basic foundation design for viewing your Joomla! website. To produce the effect of a "complete" website, the template works hand in hand with the content stored in the Joomla! databases.

This book will help you learn about how to use multiple templates in the same site. It also guides you on using animations and other effects in Joomla! templates and provides you with tricks for tweaking existing templates.

What This Book Covers

Chapter 1 will help you to brush up your web skills, especially XHTML and CSS, and help you to get ready for designing a great template for the most popular, robust, open-source content management system available for the Web today!

Chapter 2 covers the key elements of a Joomla! template and what considerations to to make while working with your mock up. You will learn some basic techniques for image extraction and optimization, and some tips and tricks to speed up the design process.

Chapter 3 will help you in setting up your development environment and an HTML editor for a smooth workflow. You will also see some of the alternatives to a full Joomla! install. You will learn about the two versions of your design—one with tables and one with semantic XHTML and CSS.

Chapter 4 will help you understand the basic wash—rinse—repeat process of debugging and validating your template's code. You will learn how to use the W3C's XHTML and CSS validation tools. You will further explore the value of using Firefox as a development tool by using its JavaScript Console and Firebug extension.

Chapter 5 talks about the `templateDetails.xml` file and what each part of that file does in detail. Also, you will learn how to package your finished template into a working ZIP file that anyone should be able to upload into their own Joomla! installation.

Chapter 6 covers the standard XHTML Markup and CSS classes for Joomla!. You will also review the standard ways to control what markup is produced via PHP and the Joomla! Administration Panel.

Chapter 7 will help you to add drop-down menus to your Joomla! template and discuss various ways to display Flash content.

In *Chapter 8*, you will look at the most popular methods to get you going with Ajax in Joomla! and to help you create interactive and dynamic forms in your Joomla! site. Also, you will see some cool JavaScripts and JavaScript toolkits that you can use to make your site appear "Ajaxy". This chapter will also help you learn how to download and install Joomla! Extensions for your Joomla! site.

Chapter 9 gives some key tips for easily implementing today's coolest CSS tricks into your template as well as a few final "fix them" tips for problems that you'll probably run into, once you turn the site over to the content editors.

Who is This Book for

This book is aimed at web designers who want to create their own unique templates for Joomla!. Readers should have a basic knowledge of Joomla! (*Building Websites with Joomla!* by Packt Publishing will help you with this) and also some knowledge of CSS and HTML, and using Dreamweaver for coding purposes.

Conventions

In this book, you will find a number of styles of text that distinguish between different kinds of information. Here are some examples of these styles, and an explanation of their meaning.

There are three styles for code. Code words in text are shown as follows: "We can include other contexts through the use of the `include` directive."

A block of code will be set as follows:

```
<html>
<head>
<title>My New Template Title</title>
</head>
<body> body parts go here </body>
</html>
```

When we wish to draw your attention to a particular part of a code block, the relevant lines or items will be made bold:

```
#header
{
    float: left;
    padding: 0px;
    margin-right: 2px;
    width: 635px;
    height: 250px;
    background: url(../images/my_nature_header.jpg) no-repeat;
}
```

New terms and **important words** are introduced in a bold-type font. Words that you see on the screen, in menus or dialog boxes for example, appear in our text like this: "clicking the **Next** button moves you to the next screen".

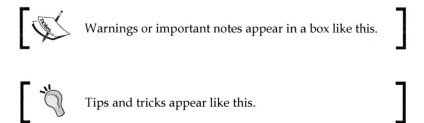

Warnings or important notes appear in a box like this.

Tips and tricks appear like this.

Reader Feedback

Feedback from our readers is always welcome. Let us know what you think about this book, what you liked or may have disliked. Reader feedback is important for us to develop titles that you really get the most out of.

To send us general feedback, simply drop an email to feedback@packtpub.com, making sure to mention the book title in the subject of your message.

If there is a book that you need and would like to see us publish, please send us a note in the **SUGGEST A TITLE** form on www.packtpub.com or email suggest@packtpub.com.

If there is a topic that you have expertise in and you are interested in either writing or contributing to a book, see our author guide on www.packtpub.com/authors.

Customer Support

Now that you are the proud owner of a Packt book, we have a number of things to help you to get the most from your purchase.

Downloading the Example Code for the Book

Visit http://www.packtpub.com/support, and select this book from the list of titles to download any example code or extra resources for this book. The files available for download will then be displayed.

The downloadable files contain instructions on how to use them.

Errata

Although we have taken every care to ensure the accuracy of our contents, mistakes do happen. If you find a mistake in one of our books—maybe a mistake in text or code—we would be grateful if you would report this to us. By doing this you can save other readers from frustration, and help to improve subsequent versions of this book. If you find any errata, report them by visiting http://www.packtpub.com/support, selecting your book, clicking on the **Submit Errata** link, and entering the details of your errata. Once your errata are verified, your submission will be accepted and the errata added to the list of existing errata. The existing errata can be viewed by selecting your title from http://www.packtpub.com/support.

Questions

You can contact us at questions@packtpub.com if you are having a problem with some aspect of the book, and we will do our best to address it.

1
Getting Started as a Joomla! Template Designer

Welcome to Joomla! template design. This book is intended to take you through the ins and outs of creating sophisticated professional templates for the Joomla! CMS. In the upcoming chapters, we'll walk through all the steps required to aid, enhance, and speed your Joomla! template design process. From design tips and suggestions to setting up your Joomla! development sandbox we'll review the best practices for coding, markup, testing, and debugging your Joomla! template, and then taking it live. The last three chapters are dedicated to additional tips, tricks, and various cookbook recipes for adding popular enhancements to your Joomla! template designs.

Let's Get Going!

If you're reading this book, chances are you currently have or work with a Joomla! powered site or are ready to embark on a new Joomla! powered project. Joomla! already comes with two built-in templates, and there are many free and commercial templates out there in a wide range of themes and styles to choose from. The benefit of using pre-existing templates (especially purchasing a commercial template) is that they're built to handle Joomla!'s range of uses and content displays. They've also been packaged and set up for easy installation and application to your project (often two clicks or less!). This means that with a little web surfing and under $100, you can have your Joomla! powered site up and running with a stylish look in no time at all.

The drawback to using a pre-made template is that you limit your site's custom look to something that several other people may have downloaded or purchased for their site. Moreover, if your site has a third-party extension for specialized content, it may not look quite right with the pre-existing template. Also, if your site requires specific branding, you may find it next to impossible to find an existing pre-made template that will fit the project's branding requirements. Thus, you'll need to either create a fresh design from scratch or dig in and modify an existing template (which has a user license that allows modification).

Whether you're working with a pre-existing template or creating a new one from the ground up, Joomla! template design will give you the know-how to effectively understand how templates work within the Joomla! CMS enabling you to have full control over your site's design and branding, no matter which route you take to get there.

Designing Templates vs. Designing Web Pages

If you are designing for the Joomla! CMS for the first time, you will need to understand that designing a template for a Content Management System such as Joomla! is quite different from designing a web page. You may be comfortable with creating a design layout in Photoshop or your favorite graphic editor and then using your editor's export feature to generate the image slices and HTML markup required to render the web page. Likewise, you may be more comfortable working with a WYSIWYG editor such as Dreamweaver so that you can clearly see your page layout as you create the CSS and format content for it.

Joomla! is different. It holds all the content within several MySQL database tables. What you'll be designing is the *shell*, which will eventually hold content when it is called from the database by a web user selecting a link on the site. At the same time, the layout and CSS you create for the template will be automatically applied across many pages (perhaps thousands) depending on how big the site is. This can be quite liberating and overwhelming, or frustrating at the same time.

The first thing you'll notice is that it will be difficult to review your Joomla! template's layout at a glance from within your local WYSIWYG editor. If you're used to working with a WYSIWYG editor to create Cascading Style Sheets for your layout, you'll notice that Joomla! generates many *id* and *class* names on-the-fly, which make it difficult (though not impossible!) to use your editor's CSS Wizard to create style sheets for Joomla!. In this book, I've taken steps where possible to let you see where it's beneficial to use your favorite graphic and WYSIWYG editors, and where it's better to "peek under the hood", and look directly at the CSS and XHTML markup we'll be creating for our templates in this book.

In a nutshell, your Joomla! template design is not the website. Joomla! has been designed to have many different templates installed so that you can quickly and easily switch between them. You can even have certain pages that call specific templates while the rest of the site calls a main template. It might be better to consider your template design as one of the many features that can be installed into the Joomla! CMS. In fact, as we work through this book, you'll notice that installing a final template package into Joomla! is almost identical to installing a module or component extension into Joomla!. Coincidence? Probably not.

Things You'll Need to Know

This book is geared towards visual designers who have no server-side scripting, programming, or manual markup experience but who are used to working with common industry standard tools like Photoshop and Dreamweaver or with other popular graphic and HTML editors. You'll be walked through clear, step-by-step instructions but there are many web development skills and Joomla! know-how that you'll need so as to gain the maximum benefit from this book.

Joomla!

Most importantly, you should already be familiar with the most current stable version of Joomla!. I used version 1.0.8 for this book, but any newer version of Joomla will have the same capabilities as 1.0.8 with some bug fixes and new features, which will be fully documented at `http://joomla.org`. You should understand how content is added to the Joomla! CMS, and how its many built-in modules and components work. Understanding the difference between a **module** (which is an extension that is smaller and lighter, normally for just one page) and a **component** (usually an extension that is much more robust and can appear across many pages) and how to install them is a plus but not necessary as we'll cover this topic in detail later in this book.

What about the new 1.5.x Beta? Yes! You can use templates made for 1.0.x Joomla! installations in the new 1.5.x Beta releases! The examples in this book have all been tested in Joomla! 1.5 Beta 2 using backwards compatibility mode. Any templates you create using the techniques in this book should work with Joomla! 1.5. While you should download, install, play with, and learn the new 1.5 Beta features (as well as post your bugs, comments, and suggestions about it to the Joomla! forums), it is *never* recommended to release anything to the public using **beta** software. For sites (especially those that have clients who are paying you and trusting you with their brand and content) always deploy Joomla! sites using the most-recent stable version. You'll always be able to upgrade your Joomla! installation once the newest beta has become stable. Remember: **new** is good as it usually means bugs from the previous version have been fixed. **Beta** means "new, never-seen-before features" or the code base has been redone from scratch and the stability of the code base for these new features has yet to be proved against bugs and hacks. For more information on the wonders of Joomla! 1.5 check out the following: http://www.joomla.org/content/view/3287/1/.

Even if you'll be working with a more technical Joomla! administrator, you should have an overview of what the Joomla! powered project you're designing entails and what, if any, additional extensions (modules and components) will be needed for the project. If your project does require additional extensions, you'll want to have them installed in your Joomla! development sandbox to ensure that your design will cover all the various types of content that the site intends to provide. Knowing how to add and edit content in Joomla! will be helpful as you'll probably want to make sure you have lots of dummy content in your sandbox in order to review how your template handles various page displays: light content, heavy content, image heavy pages, and pages generated with the additional extensions that the project requires.

First time with Joomla? I recommend you read *Building Websites with Joomla!* by Hagen Graf.

XHTML

We'll cover using WYSIWYG editors to generate your XHTML markup (and even how to convert existing templates into *whole new designs* without touching any markup at all) later, but as you'll soon see the more XHTML you know and understand, the quicker you'll be able to create well-built templates that are quick loading, expand easily to accommodate new features, and are search engine friendly.

CSS

Again, you can use WYSIWYG editors to generate CSS for your template, but throughout the course of this book, you'll find that the more comfortable you are with CSS markup and how to use it effectively with XHTML, the better your Joomla! template creating experience will be.

Beef up those web skills. I'm a big fan of the W3Schools website. If you'd like to build up your XHTML and CSS understanding, you can use this site to walk you through everything from basic introductions to robust uses of top web languages and technologies. All the lessons are easy, comprehensive, and available free at http://w3schools.com.

Not Necessary, But Helpful

If your project will be incorporating any other special technologies such as custom PHP, JavaScript, AJAX, or Flash content, the more you know and understand how those scripting languages and technologies work, the better for your template making experience (again http://w3schools.com is a great place to start). The more web technologies you have at least a general understanding of, the more likely you'll be to intuitively make a more flexible template which will be able to handle anything the Joomla! site may need to incorporate into itself in the future.

More of a visual "see it-to-do it" learner? Lynda.com has a remarkable course selection from the top CSS, XHTML/XML, JavaScript, and Flash/ActionScript people in the world. You can subscribe and take the courses online or purchase DVD-ROMs for offline viewing. The courses might seem pricey at first, but if you're a visual learner (as most designers are) it's money and time well spent. You can find out more at http://lynda.com.

Summary

To get going on your Joomla! template design, you'll want to understand how the Joomla! CMS works and have your head wrapped around the basics of the Joomla! powered project you're ready to embark on. If you'll be working with a more technical Joomla! administrator, make sure your development sandbox will have the same extensions and features the final site needs to have. You'll want to brush up on those web skills especially XHTML and CSS and get ready to embark on designing a great template for the most popular, robust, open source, content management systems available for the web today!

2
Identifying Key Elements for Design

In the world of Joomla! websites where everyone has the same modules to work with, the three main things that will differentiate your site from all the others are the color scheme, graphic element style, and module placement.

In this chapter, we will identify the key elements of a Joomla! template and discuss what considerations to make when contemplating your own design. You'll pick up some tips and tricks to help you define your color scheme and graphic style, as well as learn some standard techniques for optimizing and extracting images from your design while preparing to code it up.

We'll be working with Adobe Photoshop, but most of these techniques can be used in any image editor that has some standard filters, lets you work with layers, and create "slices" for easy image export.

 If you're on a budget and in need of a good image editor with slicing options, we recommend you use GIMP with the add-on Perlotine filter. There are a couple add-on filters for GIMP that export image slices, but the Perlotine filter has worked the best for me in the past. GIMP is free, Open Source and available for all operating systems. Get it from `http://gimp.org/`. You'll find the Perlotine add-on here: `http://registry.gimp.org/list?name=perlotine`

Creating and Reviewing the Mock-Up

In Chapter 1 we reviewed a high-level overview of what templates consist of and what the Joomla! CMS application produces at *run time* (when it loads the site with the page data into the template). We'll now look a little deeper into how those parts work together so that you can start making decisions about your template's design.

The Joomla! Template

When you install Joomla!, it comes with one or two built-in templates. In my version 1.0.8 installation, `MadeYourWeb` by Mark Hinse and `rhuk_solarflare_ii` by Rhuk, are the two available. If you have a different version, you may have different templates available to you.

We'll use the `rhuk_solarflare_ii` template to review the basic parts of a Joomla! template that you'll need to think about when you create your visual design.

First, let's look at the following figure to see how our basic template affects the Joomla! PHP output:

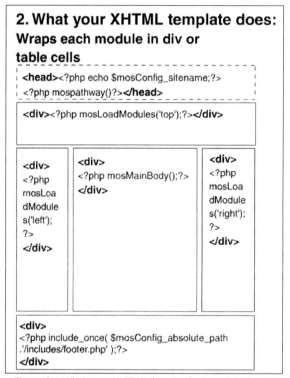

Figure 2.1 What your XHTML does to the template layout

You'll recall that the PHP code for the **footer, sitename, pathway**, and **MainBody** are not *module position* slots. These functions load in the required information that helps Joomla! to run, display standard footer information, and load the actual site content from the Joomla! MySQL databases.

Top, **left**, and **right** are *module position* slots, which can be assigned *site modules*. Site modules are what contain navigation links, form elements, and Joomla! status information that you would like to be displayed to your visitors such as: **Who's Online** or **Who's Logged In**. You can assign site modules to any of the module position slots and even load multiple site modules into these position slots by assigning an ascending numerical order to them. You do this in the **Module Manager [Site]** by going to **Modules | Site Modules** in the administration panel.

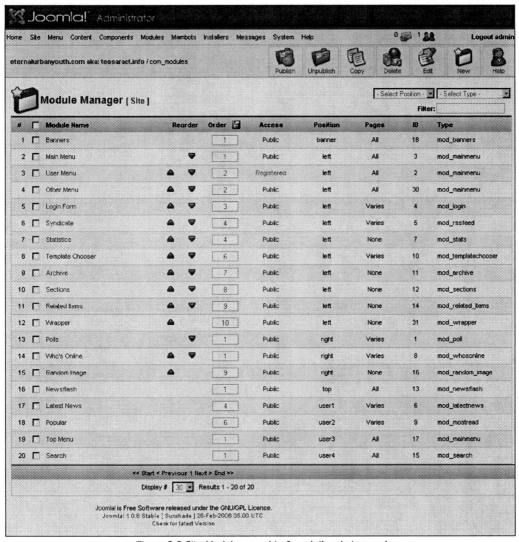

Figure 2.2 Site Modules panel in Joomla!'s admin panel

As shown in the following figure, you can assign up to 50 module position slots to place in your template layout. Go to **Site | Template Manager | Module Positions** to view the standard module positions Joomla! provides.

Figure 2.3 Module Positions panel in Joomla's admin panel

Now that we have a deeper understanding of how the template, module position slots, and site modules work, let's take a look at how these three elements come together through the `rhuk_solar_flare_ii` template. The module position slot name is on the left, the content module name is on the right, and the assigned order, if any, is underneath.

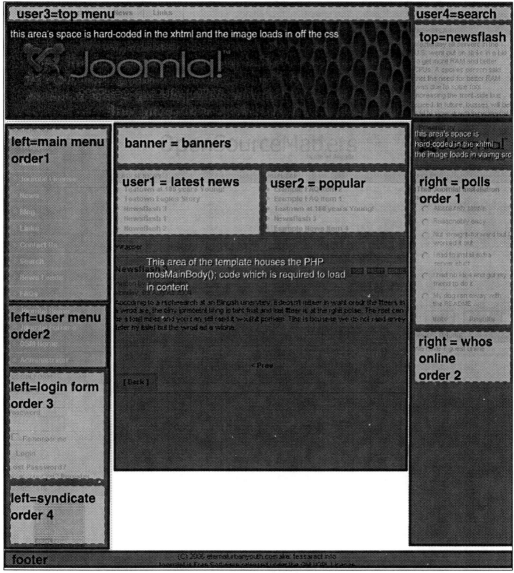

Figure 2.4 Example of modules assigned to Module Positions

Using this example, you can now start thinking of how you're going to construct your template design. Let's move on to creating your design.

Considerations to be Made

First off, let's get to the most important consideration. What modules will be used in your site? Thus, what modules do you need to design for?

Go through your Joomla! installation and review all the modules your site will be using. There's the obvious top menu, main menu, and user menus, but will you be displaying the login form or a poll? If so, do you want to change their display? Will your site be displaying banners? Will your site require any special or add-on modules or components such as an image gallery, or shopping cart?

Make a list of each module or special component that your site will be displaying and take special note of their elements: Do they have headers or special text areas? Would you like anything to be highlighted with a background image? Do the modules have items that should be standard buttons or icons? All these things should be included in your list.

When you begin work on your design in Photoshop, you'll want to compare your mock-up against your module checklist and make sure you've designed for all your modules.

Refining the Wheel

The next consideration is whether you are going to work from an existing template or from scratch? The more you work with Joomla! and learn all its quirks, the more you'll see that sometimes starting from scratch is best. However, while being a CSS and XHTML "wiz" is awesome, you don't always need to reinvent the wheel!

Take a look at what happens to the standard `rhuk` template when all we do is change the color scheme and fonts.

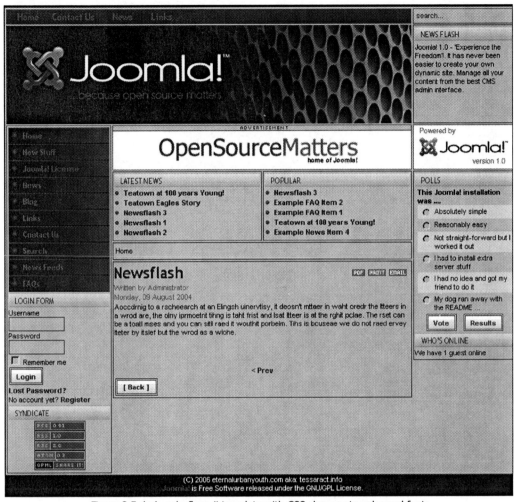

Figure 2.5 rhuk_solarflare_ii template with CSS changes to color and fonts

Now, check out what happens in the following figure when we change the graphics.

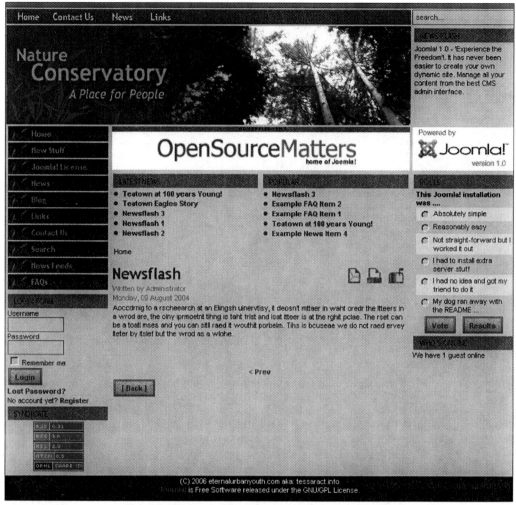

Figure 2.6 rhuk_solarflare_ii template with image changes

And last, see what happens in the following figure when we use the **Module Manager** to swap module placements around.

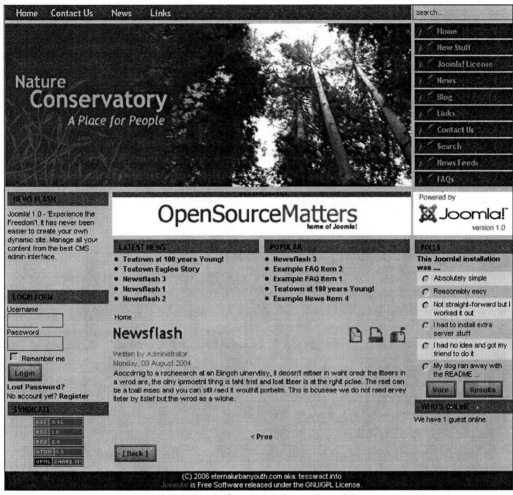

Figure 2.7 rhuk_solarflare_ii template with module swaps

By thinking of this design in terms of leveraging the existing rhuk_solarflar_ii template, we effectively created a whole new template and module layout which is completely unique. And we only had to minimally edit the CSS to get it to work. Everything else was done in the Joomla! Administration Panel without touching any code.

If you're going to work from an existing template, it's best to review that template's HTML output (right-click or *Alt*-click and chose **View Source**) and pull the image names from each page that you'll be replacing with your own images. It's also helpful to go through that template's image directory and just note each image:

which ones you're going to change, leave alone, re-size, and so on as you work with your design mock-up. Make sure to note the specific file names that are going to be overwritten in your module check list so that you have them handy when it is time to export your image slices.

So, when is it best to start from scratch? It's up to your site's specific needs. For instance, the templates Joomla! comes with use tables to hold their layout structure together. If you want an all semantic, valid XHTML markup with CSS layout, you'll need to create it yourself from scratch.

Whichever road you take, as you continue to design and build Joomla! templates, you'll find over time that you have your own "master" template—files you've generated or got to know so well—you understand how all their parts work together. You'll see how applying any new modules or components will affect the files and how they should be incorporated. It will become easy for you to work with this favorite or "master" template and "massage" it into any new creation you can imagine.

Getting the Design Rolling

The best place to start off is to define a color scheme. You'll want a predefined pallet of three to ten colors arranged in a hierarchy from most prominent to least. We would like to create a text file that lists the hex values and some comments for each color about how it should be used in the template.

 We've seen designers who do well with a scheme of only three colors, however, six to ten colors is probably more realistic for your design. Keep in mind that you've got several types of rollovers and links to deal with, and that will push your color scheme out.

Color schemes are the hardest thing to start pulling together. Designers who have many years' experience of color theory still dread coming up with eye-catching color pallets. But the fact is, it is the first thing people will notice about your site and it's the first thing that will help them notice that this is *not* another Joomla! website with some slightly varied, standard template.

Two Minute Color Schemes

When it comes to color schemes, don't sweat it. Mother Nature or at the very least, someone else, already created some of the best color schemes for us. Sure, you can just look at another site you like and see how they handled their color scheme, but it's hard to look at someone else's design and not be influenced by more than just their color scheme.

For those who intent on an original design, here's my color scheme trick. If your site will be displaying a prominent, permanent graphic or picture (most likely in the header image), start with that. If not, go through your digital photos or peruse a stock photography site and just look for pictures which appeal to you the most.

Look through the photos quickly. The smaller the thumbnails the better: content is irrelevant! Just let the photo's color hit you. Notice what you like and don't like (or what your client will like or what suites the project best) strictly in terms of color.

Pick one or two images that strike you the most and drop them into Photoshop. A thumbnail is fine in a pinch, but you'll probably want an image a bit bigger than the thumbnail. Don't use photos with a watermark, as the watermark will affect the pallet output.

Go to **Filter | Pixelate | Moziac,** and use the filter to render the image into huge pixels. The larger the cell size, the fewer colors you have to deal with, but unfortunately, the more muted the colors become.

We find that a cell size of 50 to 100 for a 72 dpi web image is sufficient. (You might need a larger cell size if your photo is of high resolution.) It will give you a nice, deep color range, and yet few enough swatches to easily pick three to ten for your site's color scheme. If you liked the image in the first place, then any of these color swatches will go together and look great! Instant color scheme.

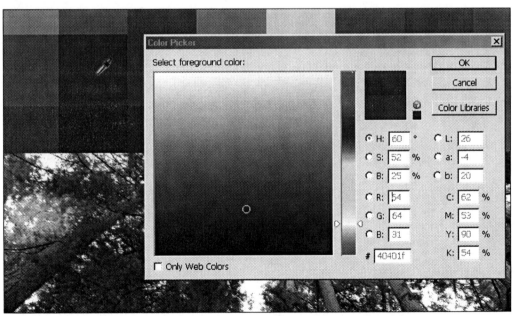

Figure 2.8 Using PhotoShop's Mozaic filter to generate a color scheme

Just pick up the eye dropper to select your favorite colors. Then double-click the foreground pallet, and copy and paste the hex number into a text file.

Keep track of this text file! It will come in handy when you're developing your mock-up design in Photoshop, and later on when you're coding in HTML and CSS.

I recommend putting little notes or comments next to the hex colors in your text files describing the color and the types of things the color is intended for — button backgrounds, rollover highlights, border edges, and so on.

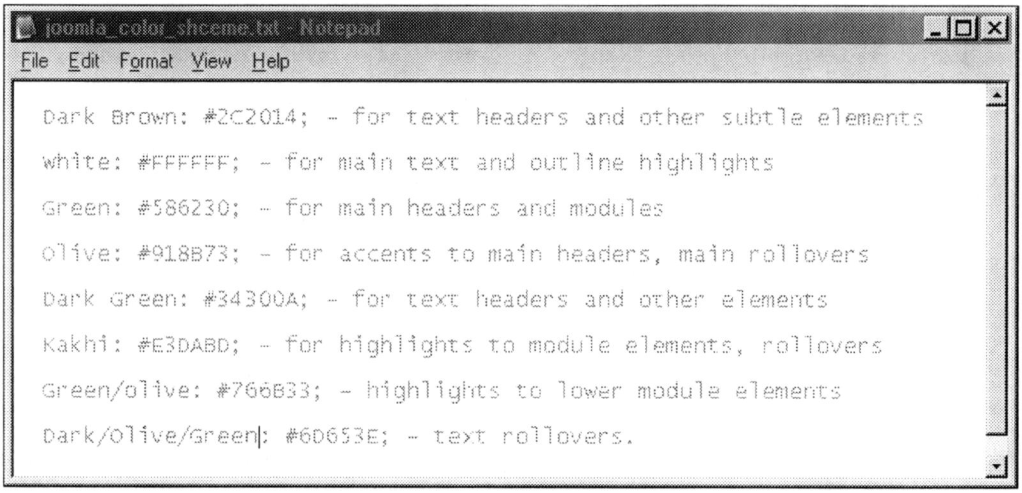

```
joomla_color_shceme.txt - Notepad                                    _ □ ×
File  Edit  Format  View  Help

Dark Brown: #2C2014; – for text headers and other subtle elements

white: #FFFFFF; – for main text and outline highlights

Green: #586230; – for main headers and modules

Olive: #918B73; – for accents to main headers, main rollovers

Dark Green: #34300A; – for text headers and other elements

Kakhi: #E3DABD; – for highlights to module elements, rollovers

Green/olive: #766B33; – highlights to lower module elements

Dark/Olive/Green: #6D653E; – text rollovers.
```

Figure 2.9 Color scheme text notes

CoffeeCup software (http://coffeecup.com) has a nifty color schemer tool. For those of you with the color theory background, this tool comes with a color wheel, color mixer, and a host of saturation, de-saturation, and other advanced tools which will provide no end to the mathematical permutations of color fun.

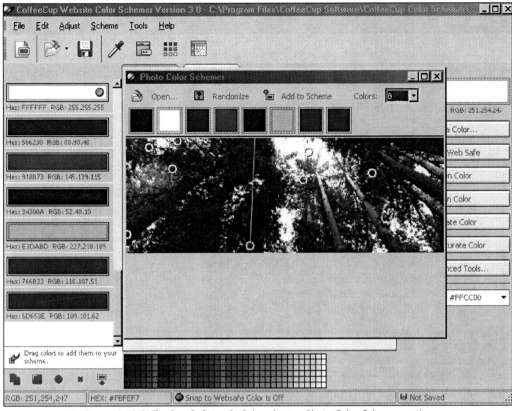

Figure 2.10 CoffeeCup Software's Colorschemer Photo Color Schemer option

We, however, prefer to use the Photo Color Schemer feature which lets us load in an eye-pleasing photo and choose 1 to 10 colors. The software's top two features include:

- Generation of the final list of your color schemes with hex, RGB, or even CMYK values, saving some precious time in copying and pasting your initial color scheme text file.

- It has a rudimentary Web Page Color Preview, which lets you drag-and-drop your swatches to a basic web-page layout and get the gist of how the colors will work best together, which we've found helpful in determining our color scheme's order of importance.

Defining the Graphic Style

You'll find Joomla! to be an icon-oriented CMS. Keeping this in mind, selecting icons, or, deciding how you want to handle Joomla!'s standard features up front, will smooth the rest of the design process as well.

We can offer you three suggestions on this front.

Invest in a good quality, royalty-free icon set which includes authoring files that you can modify as you wish (preferably, in a vector format). We like `http://www.iconbuffet.com` and `http://stockicons.com`, but a quick Google search will turn up many more. (Be sure you read the royalty-free agreement and have proper usage rights and rights to modify the icon set you purchase.)

- Find your icons at `http://openclipart.org`. Open Clip Art offers illustrations in a native vector SVG format. They're easy to edit into your own creations with a vector or image editor.

- Don't use icons! The built-in `rhuk` template, just uses standard grey squares with the words — pdf, email, print, and so on in them. There's no reason why you can't do the same.

 If you don't have a vector editor such as Adobe Illustrator, Inkscape (`http://inkscape.org`) is a great open source SVG vector editor and what many artists who contribute to `openclipart.org` use.

The icons (or standard buttons) you choose, and the way you choose to treat them can be used as a guide for how to handle the rest of your template's elements.

Are your icons cartoony with bold lines? You'll then want to repeat that effect in other site elements, such as making sure navigation buttons or header backgrounds have their edges outlined. Are they somewhat photo realistic? Are they with drop shadows or reflections? Again, you'll want to think of ways to subtly repeat those elements throughout your site. This is a simple detail, but it brings a template design together, looking sharp and highly professional.

Again, we recommend you make a list and take notes during this process. If you apply a style to an icon and reuse it somewhere in your design, make a note of it so that you can reference it for future elements. For example: "All background header images, while being of different colors for different uses, get the 'iMac' highlight applied to them as used in the main icon set. Use custom action pallet "iMacMe". Or "All side elements have a bottom border with a color that fades up with a 90 degree gradient path."

No matter how well you plan the layout in your mock-up phase, you may later on find (especially while coding) that there's an element you need to go back and design for. Having a style list for your elements will become an invaluable time saver. You'll have something to reference and won't waste time figuring out how the module element should be styled in relation to other similar elements or how you created a particular style effect.

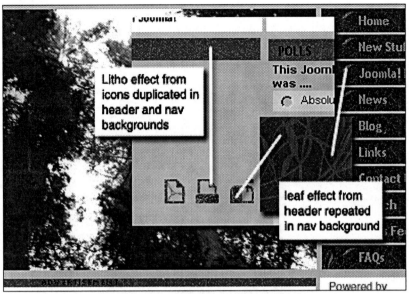

Figure 2.11 Detail of rhuk_solarflare_ii template

Slice 'n' Dice

At this point, you know what modules you have to design, and you've thought about whether you're going to start from scratch or modify an existing template. You should have your color scheme and graphic styles defined and applied to your template's mock-up in an image file.

It's now time to start considering what parts of your mock-up get exported for the template and what parts are going to be all code.

If you're used to standard WYSIWYG or Photoshop Slice n' Dice design, you've got a little more to think about. You can't just slice your image up and export it with an HTML page. Joomla! templates don't work like that. Content is separate from layout. The majority of your images will need to be loaded using CSS.

You'll need to look at your design and start thinking in terms of what will be exported as a complete image, and what will be used as a background image. You'll probably find that your header image is the only thing that will be sliced whole. Many of your background images should be sliced so that their size is optimized for use as a repeated image.

If you notice that an image can repeat horizontally to get the same effect, then you'll only need to slice a small vertical area of the image. Same goes for noticing images that can repeat vertically. You'll only need to slice a small horizontal area of the image and set the CSS repeat rule to load in the image.

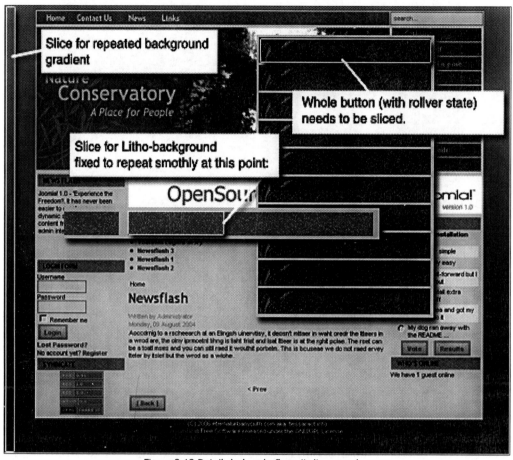

Figure 2.12 Detail rhuk_solarflare_ii slice samples

If you'd like more information on how to slice and work with background images, repeating and non-repeating for use with CSS, check out this article from adobe's site:

http://www.adobe.com/devnet/dreamweaver/articles/
css_bgimages.html

Your menu items will need to be exported as background images without graphic text. Joomla! generates the text for each link dynamically so it's best to style that text with CSS and have an eye-catching background image with one image that includes its rollover beneath it. Same goes for section headers, if you'd like them graphically highlighted, it's best to export a background image so that the dynamically generated html text can be displayed over the image.

 Wellstyled.com has an excellent tutorial on how to use a single image technique to handle image background rollovers with CSS.

`http://wellstyled.com/css-nopreload-rollovers.html`

Now that you've placed the slices for each of your template image elements, export them using the smallest compression options available, and get ready to look at some code.

If you're working from an existing template and overwriting images, pull out that module check list, and make sure that each slice is correctly named and assigned the same file type so it will overwrite the old template image.

Putting It All Together

At this point you should have the following:

1. Module checklist—listing all the elements your design will handle
   - Image checklist—(if you're going to leverage an existing template structure) list of all image names, sizes, and what modules they belong to
2. Color scheme hex list—a list of your hex values for copying and pasting into your image layout and code
3. Graphic-style notes—a list of things you've done to your icons and standard ways to treat repeating graphic elements
4. Full mock-up layout
5. Sliced and exported images

Summary

In this chapter, we covered the key elements of a Joomla! template and what considerations to make when working with your mock up. We went over some basic techniques for image extraction and optimization as well as covered some tips and tricks to speed up the design process. You should now have your color scheme hex values defined and listed in a handy text file, and your key image elements optimized and exported into their own images. We're now ready to take on our template. Let's get coding!

3
Coding It Up

We are now ready to take our visual design and make it a reality. We'll start by continuing the process suggested in Chapter 2 and apply our new design to a copy of the existing `rhuk_solarflare_ii` template.

We'll them discuss the importance of semantic XHTML and show you how to create our new design from scratch, eliminating as many tables as possible, and using all XHTML and CSS, for a fast-loading, SEO-friendly template.

First, let's make sure you've got some basics set up to handle a standard workflow for your template creation. You'll need a hosted or local version of Joomla! and a good HTML editor. Most of you will be using Dreamweaver, which we'll cover here, although any HTML or text editor that lets you see the line number on the left of the screen would be ideal. If the editor lets you view code in color context for HTML tags, attributes, CSS rules, and PHP function variables and strings, that's even better!

We will do our best to show you as much as possible through the WYSIWYG and wizard views of the editors, but there are going to be many steps where it will be necessary to edit the PHP code, CSS, and XHTML directly. I'll be as thorough as possible in these steps to ensure that everyone has a positive experience while hitting the **view code** or **source tab** button in their editor of choice.

Need a visual editor equivalent to Dreamweaver or GoLive? We recommend Nvu `http://nvu.com` or KompoZer `http://kompozer.net`. KompoZer is a more recent fork from Nvu's code base and does have some bug fixes in it that Nvu hasn't released yet. Both Nvu and KompoZer are based on Mozilla's Composer code base.

Already know the code? Then use a text-based editor like HTML-kit `http://www.chami.com/HTML-kit/`. HTML-kit is not open-source, but it's still free and has a large community of plug-in developers, which enables HTML-kit to support several types of validation and all your favorite scripting languages.

Got Joomla!?

First things first! If by some chance you don't have one yet, you'll need an installation of Joomla! to work with. You can build your template "blind", only working locally in your HTML editor. But as you'll see, we'll be restricted from pure WYSIWYG work, so we do need a way to see our template in action as it progresses. Also, in some instances we'll be using Joomla!'s Administration Panel to help place modules and components as well as control how module content is being output.

As we explained in Chapter 1, we assume you're familiar with Joomla! and its administration basics and have a development installation to work with. If you need help in getting your Joomla! installation up and running, or need an overview of how to use the Joomla! Administration Panel, we highly recommend you to read Packt Publishing's *Building Websites with Joomla!* by Matjaz Juric, Sohail Salehi, and Hagen Graf.

Joomla! Servers

For those of you already familiar with Joomla!, we have a couple of standalone Joomla! installs to recommend for template development.

If you don't have a web server available to you at all, we highly recommend Ravenwood Joomla! Server (formerly called JoomlaLite).

```
http://extensions.joomla.org/component/option,com_mtree/
task,listcats/cat_id,1850/Itemid,35/
```

Ravenwood Joomla! Server is probably the easiest development installation to get rolling, and it allows you to run Joomla! on your local machine without a web server. In fact, if you have a web server running on your computer, like Apache or IIS, you must disable it (likewise for MySQL) for Ravenwood JS to work properly.

Ravenwood JS is so light that you can even run it from an external flash/USB drive. This enables you to have multiple versions of Joomla! installs for different projects (but you can only run one installation at a time), and take a project with you from computer to computer.

Another alternative is to use **JSAS (Joomla! Stand Alone Server)**. JSAS is somewhat similar to Ravenwood JS, but it's a bit bigger (and probably won't fit on a flash drive). However, it lets you have five separate Joomla! sites under one installation.

```
http://www.joomla.org/content/view/462/37/
```

Mac users: You will need to rely on an installation of Joomla! on a server, or you can install XAMPP for Mac OSX. Afterwards, you'll need to run a full installation of Joomla!.

`http://www.apachefriends.org/en/xampp-macosx.html`

You can also just install PHP and MySQL individually on your Mac, and then install Joomla! again using the handy instructions from `macjoomla.com`:

`http://www.macjoomla.com/articles/joomla/`
`install_joomla_on_your_mac.html`

WYSIWYG Editors:
What-You-See-Isn't-Really-What-You-Get

So you are more used to Dreamweaver, GoLive, or some other neat WYSIWYG editor rather than a plain-text editor. Maybe you make your designs in Photoshop or Fireworks and hit the **Save for Web** feature that outputs your slices into clean, compressed images along with an HTML page. You can then open up that HTML page in your WYSIWYG HTML editor and see everything. You make a few more tweaks, add your page text and maybe some links, hit **Save** again, and upload your HTML page and image directory to the server. Why can't we just do that here?

The Joomla! CMS, like all good content management systems (including blog tools), keeps its content completely separate from the design. The menus and text are not anywhere in the template's page. All the page content, menu items, and module displays are stored in the "ether of cyberspace" known as Joomla!'s MySQL database tables. All the template's image elements are dealt with in its CSS file (`template_css.css`).

The average Joomla! `index.php` template page (if it's built right) has *nothing visual in it*, save a few table cells! The design images are not hard coded into the HTML tables as they are when you export a sliced image with an HTML page from Photoshop or GIMP.

This makes working with and developing templates in a WYSIWYG environment quite challenging. Take a look at what the `rhuk_solarflare_ii` template looks like in the **Design** view of Dreamweaver:

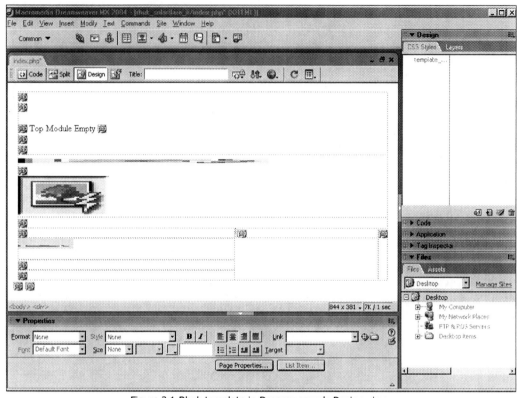

Figure 3.1 Rhuk template in Dreamweaver's Design view.

Even when we (temporarily) associate the Rhuk template with its CSS sheet, it's still not much to look at:

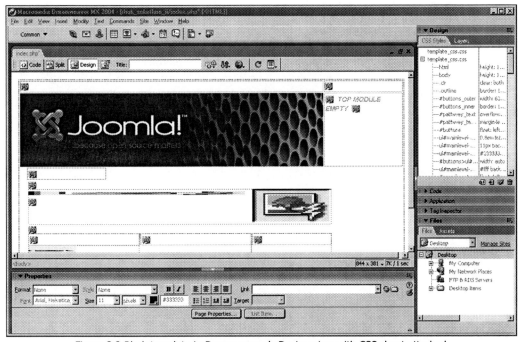

Figure 3.2 Rhuk template in Dreamweaver's Design view with CSS sheet attached.

Not very helpful visually! You may be thinking: "I've heard of Joomla! extensions for HTML editors; maybe one of those is all I need". Yes, you are right. There are extensions out there to help you with your Joomla! template creation.

You'll find extensions for Dreamweaver and HTML-kit here:

`http://mamboxchange.com/frs/?group_id=106&release_id=1801`

There's also an extension for Nvu here (though, it does appear to be in beta):

`http://mamboxchange.com/frs/?group_id=1509`

 You should be aware that the Joomla! HTML editor extensions basically help you since you do not have to remember specific PHP code for content and module positions.

Even while using extensions, you will be spending the majority of your time in the **Code** view of the HTML editor, placing your cursor where you want the PHP code for the module position to appear, and then selecting your code of choice from the extension drop-down menu.

Also, most extensions are originally written for Mambo, not Joomla!. While at the moment, they are compatible with Joomla! 1.0.x installs, as time goes, unless someone comes up with an all-Joomla! extension (I'm sure they will, but at this time I couldn't find one), the module position code may change, rendering your extension useless with future releases of Joomla!.

In the course of this chapter, you won't need to use an extension as we will be getting very intimate with the template's header, content, footer, and module position's PHP code. We strongly recommend that you take this opportunity to learn and understand how these pieces work within the template first.

Once you have a general understanding of what each piece of code will produce, using a Joomla! extension for your editor will streamline your workflow, preventing you from constantly hunting and pecking through your previous template endeavors for code snippits to cut and paste.

Extensions! Make your own code repository. Now that you know the low-down on how template extensions work, any good editor, be it WYSIWYG or text-based, has what's usually called a "snippits panel" (Sometimes this is just a folder that's part of your working directory view.) This feature enables you to create a code snippit or page in which you copy and paste your own reusable code or text. The application will remember it forever and keep it readily available for reuse, usually via a single click or key stroke. Some editors will even let you drag-and-drop the code to its rightful place in your template. If you don't have this feature in your editor, or you just want something robust, you can use inteleXual's Yankee Clipper III (I personally use it) http://www.intelexual.com/products/YC3/. YC3 isn't open-source, but it is a free and a very powerful standalone application that you can use with more than just your HTML editor.

Setting Up Your Workflow

Your workflow will pretty much look like the following:

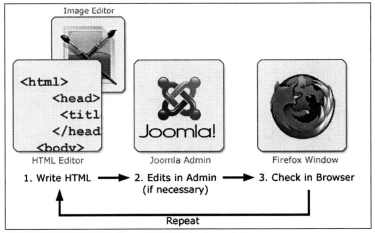

Figure 3.3 Your basic work-flow

You'll be editing CSS and XHTML in your HTML editor. After each edit, hit **Save**, then *Alt+tab* or taskbar over to your browser window, and hit **Refresh** to check the results. (I would usually direct you to use *Alt+tab*, but you can use different ways provided you get to the desired window.) Depending on where you are in this process, you might also have two or more browser windows or tabs open: one with your Joomla! template view and others with the various Joomla! Administration Panels that you're using.

Dreamweaver, Nvu, or a robust text editor like HTML-kit all let you FTP directly via a site panel or set up a working directory panel (if you're working locally with a standalone server). *Be sure to use this feature.* It will let you edit and save to the actual index.php file and the template_css.css style sheet without having to stop and copy to your working directory or uploading your file with a standalone FTP client. You will then be able to *Alt+tab* to a browser and view your results instantly after hitting **Save**.

Be sure to save regularly and take backups! Backups are sometimes more important than saving. They enable you to roll back to a previously stable version of your design if your XHTML and CSS have stopped playing nice. Rather than continuing to futz with your code, wondering where you broke it, it's sometimes much more cost-effective to roll back to your last good stopping point and try again. You can set your preferences in some editors, like HTML-kit, to auto save backups for you in a directory of your choice. However, only you know when you're at a good "Hey, this is great!" spot. When you get to these points, get into the habit of using the **Save a Copy** feature to take backups. Your future-futzing-self will love you for it.

Firefox: Use It

One more workflow issue before we get to the fun stuff. Note that the browser icon in Figure 3.3 is a Firefox icon. It's more than a suggestion, or just what I, as a geek prefer. It's what you should use when developing for the Web, period.

If you don't like Firefox, then you can temporarily get away with using something else like Opera, or maybe Safari (if you're on a Mac). But you really should be using Firefox.

 Please, do not use Internet Explorer with your template-development process.

I know that you're thinking that I simply don't like IE. But this is not the case at all, IE6 can easily slip into what's called **quirks mode,** where, for whatever reason, it works more like old IE 5.x browsers and simply does not render CSS quite the same way that all the other W3C-compliant browsers in the world do.

While IE 7 is reportedly going to handle most of these CSS rendering issues, and maybe you are already using IE 7, I'm just not 100 percent convinced, especially as IE 7 will probably still run differently if quirks mode is triggered.

The main reason why I recommend Firefox is because it is truly a designer and developer's browser. Firefox has great features that we'll be taking advantage of to help us streamline our development process. In addition to these built-in features, Firefox has a host of extremely useful extensions that I'll recommend to further enhance your workflow.

The secondary reason to use Firefox is back to IE. Yes, you are thinking "But everyone uses IE and knows about its quirks mode CSS rendering issues, so why not just design for it?" And that is exactly what we'll be doing.

Why exactly must we design for Firefox first, then IE? Because IE's quirks are so well-known among web designers and developers, there are tons of well-documented hacks and workarounds for them. However, if you set up your design only viewing it so that it looks good in IE first, and then check it out in Firefox and other browsers to find it a mess, wrangling with your CSS rules at that point will be much more difficult. Think: driving backwards with no back window or side mirrors in a snow storm.

It will be much easier for you if you develop for Firefox first with valid XHTML and CSS code. The ideal scenario will be that your markup will remain valid and not trigger IE's quirks mode, saving you a lot of CSS problems. However, if for some reason, your template triggers quirks mode in IE, then you'll still be able to go in and sparingly apply a well-documented hack or workaround here and there to compensate for IE's quirks-mode-related box-model issues, pixel drift, and all the other common rendering anomalies known to IE and its quirks mode. The end result will be a valid template that looks great in all browsers.

In a nutshell, there's no need to view usage of Firefox as part of picking sides in the "Microsoft vs. the World" saga. Firefox is just another good development tool, like your image editor, HTML editor, checklists, and FTP client. When you're not developing, you can use whatever browser you prefer.

Let's Make a Template

We're going to continue leveraging the `rhuk_solarflare_ii` template. Open your HTML editor, and set it up to display a FTP or local working directory panel so that you have access to your Joomla! installation files. Also, have a couple of browser windows or tabs open with your Joomla! home page loaded into them as well as having the Joomla! Administration Panel available.

Tabs: Use them. They're one of those neat built-in Firefox features I was talking about. Keep all your Joomla! development and administrator views in one window. Each tab within a Firefox window is accessible via *Ctrl+1, Ctrl+2,* ... keystrokes. It makes for a much cleaner workspace, especially because we will already be in constant *Alt+tab* flip mode. Flipping to the wrong browser windows gets annoying and slows you down. You will quickly get in the habit of using "*Alt+tab* or *Ctrl+number?*" to jump right to your Joomla! template, your Joomla! Administration page, and so on.

To get started, we'll create a copy of the existing Rhuk template. I'm using a development installation of Joomla! on a remote server via FTP. If you're working locally, you can follow my instructions using common desktop commands instead of an FTP client.

1. Inside your Joomla! installation, locate the template directory and make a copy of the `rhuk_solarflare_ii` directory. Save this to your desktop or local working directory. (I've blurred out the files sitting on my desktop so that they don't distract you.)

2. Rename the copy of the directory to a template name that suits your project (and copy it back to the server if working remotely). You'll see in Figure 3.4, I've renamed my directory: **my_nature_design** and I'm uploading it to my Joomla! templates directory.

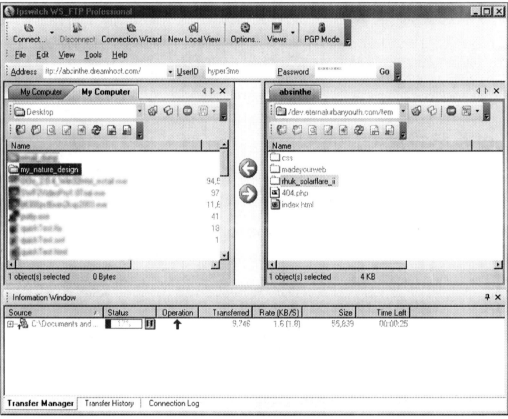

Figure 3.4 Renaming the Rhuk template

3. Use *Alt+tab* to go over to your Joomla! Administration Panel and look at the **Template Manager** view. Go to **Site | Template Manager | Site Templates**. You'll notice that there are now *two* `rhuk_solarflare_ii` templates displayed.

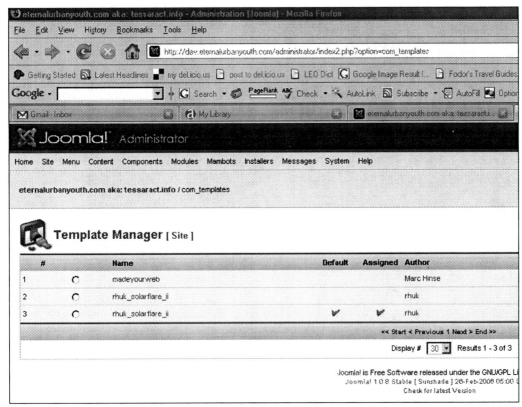

Figure 3.5 Admin panel

4. Use *Alt+tab* to go over to your HTML editor and open the `templateDetails.xml` file from inside the new template directory. At the top of the page, between the opening and closing `name` tags, write in the new name of your template design. This should be the **exact same name** you already named the directory `my_nature_design`. If you want, you can update the other basic information in the XML file, but the `name` tag change is all that is required at this time. Hit **Save.** Our code in the `templateDetails.xml` file looks like this:

```
<name>my_nature_design</name>
```

5. *Alt+tab* over to the **Template Manger** view, and hit **Refresh**. You will see the copy of the Rhuk template, now has your new name displayed in the **Template Manager** view.

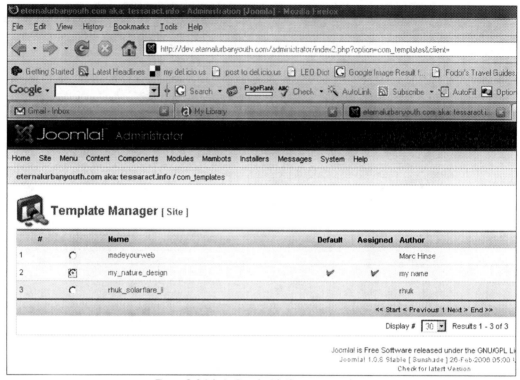

Figure 3.6 Admin Panel with the new template

6. Select the new template's radio button and use the **Template Manager** view's **Default** and **Assign** buttons (in the upper-right corner) to make your new copy the *default, assigned* template to Joomla!. After clicking the **Default** button, you should click the **Assign** button. This will assign all the pages of your new template (just select them all for now). Then click the **Save** icon.

There's one more step needed to make sure our new template copy is ready to go.

7. In your HTML editor, open the `index.php` file. You will have to look at it in **Code** view. Note that, approximately on the *43rd* line, you will need to replace the `rhuk_solarflare_ii` directory name with the new directory name you gave your template right before the `template_css.css` name. This ensures the template is referencing the new style sheet. The `href` code should look like the following:

```
<?php echo $mosConfig_live_site;?>
/templates/your_new_template_name/css/template_css.css
```

Making Changes to Your New Template

Now that our template base is ready, let's make a dramatic change to it. Our first change will actually be through the Joomla! Administration Panel. We already know that we're going to be moving the main navigation buttons from the left module position slot to the top module position slot.

1. Login and select **Modules | Site Modules.** You will then be in the **Module Manager** screen.

2. Scroll down and click **Main Menu.** You'll then be in the **Site Module: Edit [Main Menu]** screen.

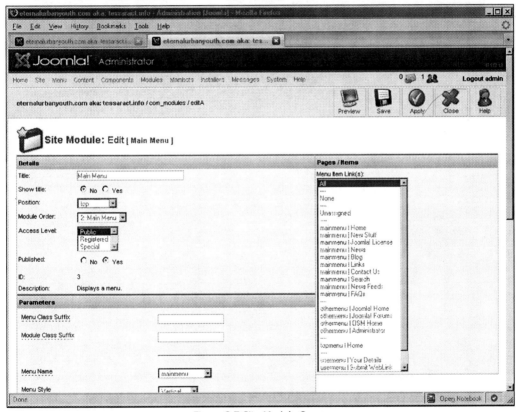

Figure 3.7 Site Module Screen

3. Click the **No** radio button next to **Show Title.** We want to turn off the title for this module in our design, as we're pretty sure people will understand it's the main menu.

4. Select **top** from the drop-down list next to **Position.**

5. Select **Apply** from the top menu.

6. Use *Alt+tab* to go over to your browser template view, and then **Refresh**. Your layout should now look something like the following:

Figure 3.8 First look at your Joomla Template Layout

So far so good! You can see, however, that the height of the top module position doesn't allow all our navigation buttons to show up. Let's fix that. Here's where Firefox comes in handy. We will be using the **DOM Source of Selection** inspector (that's one of the HTML views of the web page available in Firefox) to find out what CSS rule is affecting the top module's height.

7. Use *Alt+tab* to go over to your Joomla! template view, and select the text of the available main menu buttons. Make sure that you select some text above and/or below the main menu buttons. This will ensure that you capture all the relevant tags to the menu.

8. Right-click and select **View Selection Source**. This will open up a window that lets you see Firefox's DOM Source of Selection inspector for just the items you've selected.

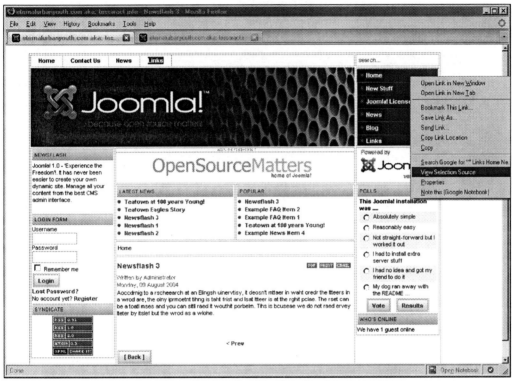

Figure 3.9 Selecting View Selection Source

9. View the DOM Source of Selection, and locate the main menu items. (If you find the code confusing to look at, just press *Ctrl+F* to find the menu items **Home** or **New Stuff**. This will put you in the right area of the code and then just look a few lines up from Home.)

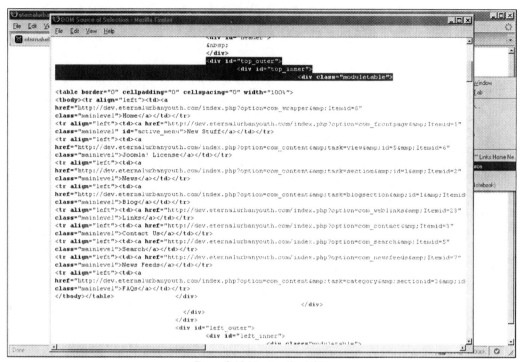

Figure 3.10 Viewing the DOM

10. Note that, just above the table where the main menu items start, there are two `div` ids and one class reference that is affecting our `top` module position layout. It is likely that one of these ids or the class rule is what's affecting our `top` module position height. Again, just as in Chapter 2, you'll find it very useful to have a scratch text pad open so that you can make checklists and notes.

11. Copy down the two id names `top_outer`, `top_inner` and the class name: `moduletable` somewhere where you will be able to easily reference them later.

We're now ready to take a look at the `template_css.css` style sheet. If you're familiar with CSS rule syntax, go ahead and open up the `template_css.css` from inside the CSS directory into your HTML editor. It should open right into **Code** or **Source** view. If not, make sure you're in **Code** view so that you can see all the rules.

If you're more comfortable using your HTML editor's CSS Wizard, we recommend that you float the CSS styles panel and CSS properties panel next to each other in Dreamweaver so that each rule that you click on in the styles panel will appear next to it in the properties panel as I've done in Figure 3.11.

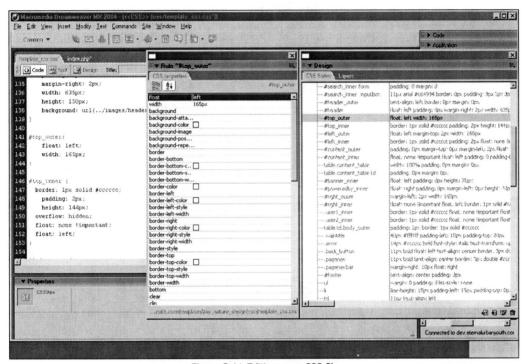

Figure 3.11 Editing your CSS file

Try to use the Code view Overall, I recommend that as much as possible, you should go ahead and work directly in the style sheet's **Code** view. The wizard views are a good way to see what's going on in your style sheet, and the **Properties** panel can help jog your memory for the syntax and spellings of various CSS properties. But if you know that you're just going to change a hex color, or a pixel height or width, go ahead and look directly at the CSS sheet in the **Code** view. Otherwise, you may accidentally add or delete properties. Sometimes even accidentally adding blank properties in a rule can detrimentally affect the layout's outcome, depending on how the rule is applied. Dreamweaver and many other CSS wizards will let you right-click on a selected rule in the **Styles** panel and **Go to the Code** or **View Code**, effectively taking you right to the correct spot in the **Code** view of the style sheet. This is a good way to become more familiar with your style sheets through the CSS wizard, while ensuring that all your edits are the intended ones and are done directly in the **Code** view.

Looking at our style sheet or in the **Style** panel, let's find those two ids and class names and have a look at them.

It's just a good design practice to name CSS rules that affect only a particular module position with that module position's name. You will speed your workflow and be much less confused in the long run. It's clear that the Rhuk template designer followed this practice, so it's clear that the `moduletable` class is not what we're looking for. We want to edit one of the `top_outer` or `top_inner` classes.

The Difference between CSS Classes and IDs

In general, classes are not used to denote position, height, width, or other main features of module positions. (Classes have a "`.`" before their name in a style sheet and can be reused by *many* different XHTML elements on a page using the `class` attribute.) Because each module position should be unique within your template, you will only ever have one `top` module, one `left` module, one `right` module and so on, so it makes sense to use only ids to control module positions. (Ids have a "#" before their name and can only be assigned to *one* XHTML object on the page using the `id` attribute.)

Since we're looking to change the height of the `top` module, it's pretty clear that either the `top_outer` or `top_inner` ids is where we need to look because they have got the word `top` in their name, and they are ids, not classes.

Let's look at the first id rule: `top_outer`. It turns out that `top_outer` only has two properties associated with it, and neither of them are the `height` property. So let's look at `top_inner`.It is set to a `height` of `144px`.

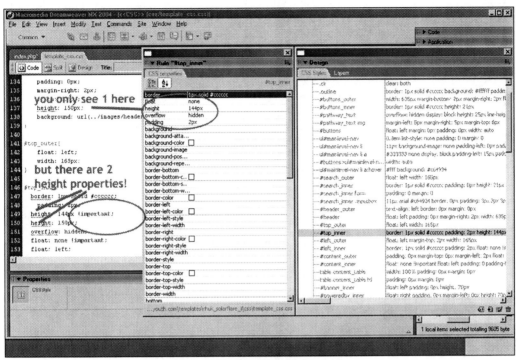

Figure 3.12 Editing the top_inner rule

That's what the **Properties** panel shows. If we look in the actual style sheet using the **Code** view, we see that `top_inner` actually has *two* `height` properties! (This is another good reason for trying to work inside the **Code** view as much as possible.) The second `height` property has a value of `150px`. The Rhuk template author has added the `!important` property value as a *hack* after the first `height` property, so the layout will render well in Firefox and IE.

!important They don't call them Cascading Style Sheets for nothing! Using the !imporant property value is one of the most common ways to hack IE. Normally, whatever rule is last specified in a style sheet takes precedence. Hence, the style sheet *cascades*. However, if you use !important after a property value, then that CSS property will take precedence regardless of what appears after it. This is true for *all browsers* except IE, which completely ignores it. If IE has fallen into quirks mode, borders, margins, and padding property values, will start to get off compared to Firefox. (We'll look at the box model that describes this in detail in Chapter 4, *Debugging and Validation*.) If your height property looks good at 144px in Firefox, but needs to be set to 150px to accommodate IE's issues, then you can see how setting a Firefox height property *first* with a !important value will make it look good in Firefox and other compliant browsers while IE ignores it and picks up the last height value, looking great at 150px.

Checking our design mock-up in our image editor, we can see that we will need about 250 pixels to accommodate our main menu's height. We can also see, based on the Rhuk's design, that there must be about a six pixel difference between Firefox and IE due to some other margins or padding. So let's enter 250px into the *first* height property with the !important value and enter 256px into the *second* height property. The code should look like this:

```
#top_inner {
    padding: 2px;
    height: 250px !important;
    height: 256px;
    overflow: hidden;
    float: none !important;
    float: left;
}
```

Hit **Save,** use *Alt-tab* to go over to your template's browser view, and **Refresh.**

Figure 3.13 Checking the menu height

This is looking good. All the menu items are visible and the padding is consistent. (This would be one of those ideal moments to *save* a *backup!*)

At this point, I'll assume based on my previous explanation and images, that you understand how to use Firefox's DOM Source of Selection inspector to locate the id and class names of XHTML elements that you'd like to manipulate via their CSS rules.

From here on in this chapter, I'll just reference the id or class name that we're changing and not drag you through its location finding process. I'll also assume that you will be working with your CSS sheet the way you're most comfortable. Just be aware that, if you're working in the CSS wizard view, you may inadvertently add or remove code or miss hacks and workarounds added by the Rhuk author.

Changing Our Template Colors

Remember all those lists we made in Chapter 2? They will be coming in handy. Open up your color palette text file and have it ready. We're going to start changing the colors in our template.

1. Use *Alt+tab* to go over to your HTML editor viewing your CSS sheet.

2. Find the `outline` id rule in the style sheet and change the `background` property to your main content area background color. In our case, it's `#e3dabd`. It should look like the following:

```
outline {
    border: 1px solid #586230;
    background: #e3dabd;
    padding: 2px;
}
```

3. Use *Alt+tab* to go over to your template browser, hit **Refresh**, and check. The inner table areas of the content should be the light-beige, `#e3dabd` color.

4. Find the `body` rule in the `template_css.css` style sheet, and add the `background` property to it. Place in your color palette's main background color. Our background color is `#070706`. It should look like the following:

```
body {
    height: 100%;
    margin-bottom: 1px;
    background: #070706;
}
```

5. Use *Alt+tab* to go over to your template browser, **Refresh**, and check:

Figure 3.14 Checking the background property

Whoops! Something has gone wrong. Our background color *didn't change* when we added the `background` property. Look at the style sheet again and notice that there are two `body` element rules. (The second `body` rule appears at line 323!) We're not sure why the Rhuk author did that. Let's consolidate these two `body` element rules.

1. Find the last body rule at about line 323 in the `template_css.css` style sheet, select and copy it's properties, and then delete the rule.

2. Move up to the first body rule and paste the new properties under the existing ones. You will now have two `height` properties set to 100%. You can delete one of them.

3. Move the `margin-bottom` property underneath the `margin` property. Again, the last property wins, so the 15 pixel "all margins" property would overwrite the 1 pixel `margin-bottom` property.

4. Change the background color to your color pallet's main background color. (Again ours is #070706.) You should now have a single body rule at line 7 of the template_css.css sheet that looks like the following:

```
body {
    height: 100%;
    margin: 15px;
    margin-bottom: 1px;
    padding: 0px;
    font-family: Arial, Helvetica, Sans Serif;
    line-height: 120%;
    font-size: 11px;
    color: #333333;
    background: #070706;
}
```

5. Use *Alt+tab* to go over to your template browser view and check:

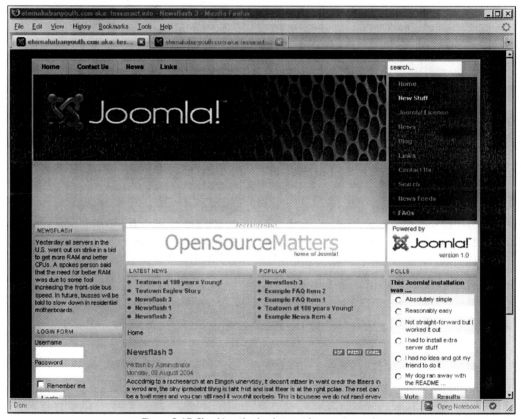

Figure 3.15 Checking the background property again

OK, looks good. Let's continue changing the colors. After each id change, we will assume you're Alt+tabbing and checking the results in your browser. We will continue using our colors, fonts, and pixel spacing but feel free to interchange any property value we denote with a property value that matches your own template design.

6. Add the `background` property to the `buttons_inner` rule and set it to `#586230`.

7. Change the `border` property color on the `outline` rule to `#586230`.

For our template design, we want to get rid of almost all the grey outlines separating each module position. The only outlines we'd like to keep are the outlines surrounding the **Login**, **Back**, **Vote**, and **Result**-type buttons. We can see several rules touting the same `border: 1px solid #cccccc;` property.

We will press *Ctrl+F* and use our HTML editor's "find" feature to zero in on each `border` property with those values and see, one by one, if they're something we want to remove, or change the color to the dark green of our color scheme.

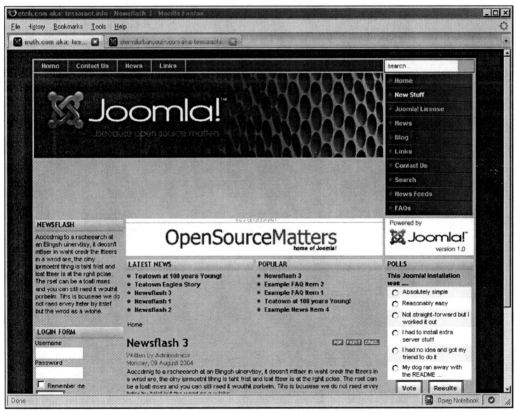

Figure 3.16 Checking the border change

Now that we've removed each of the unwanted outlines, let's move on to the final rollover colors and fonts.

1. Find the `ul#mainlevel-nav li a:hover` rule. Change the `background` property color to `#e3dabd`. This fixes the rollover on the top menu.

2. Change the `color` property of the `ul#mainlevel-nav li a:hover` rule to `#e3dabd` and add a `font-family` property of `Trebuchet MS, Helvetica, Arial` to it as well.

3. Change the `color` property of the `ul#mainlevel-nav li a:hover` rule to `#586230`. This makes the fonts and rollover colors of the top menu work with our color scheme.

4. Find the `a:link, a:visited` rule. Change the `color` property to `#586230`.

5. Find the `a:hover` rule. Change the `color` property to `#918B73`.

6. Add a `font-family` property of `Trebuchet MS, Helvetica, Arial` to the `contentheading` rule. Then change the color to `#586230`.

7. Add a `font-family` property of `Trebuchet MS, Helvetica, Arial` to the `table.moduletable th, div.moduletable h3` rule. Then change the color to `#586230`. Increase the `font-size` property to `12`.

Figure 3.17 Checking the fonts

Changing and Adding New Images to Our Template

Now we're ready to add our images. In Chapter 2, we were careful to export most of our images using the same name and image type as the images in the Rhuk template. The only image to which we gave a unique name was our header image. For the most part, we should just be able to upload (or copy if working locally) our images into our new template's image directory and let them overwrite the existing Rhuk images.

While you do this, press *Alt+tab* and **Refresh** to check your template.

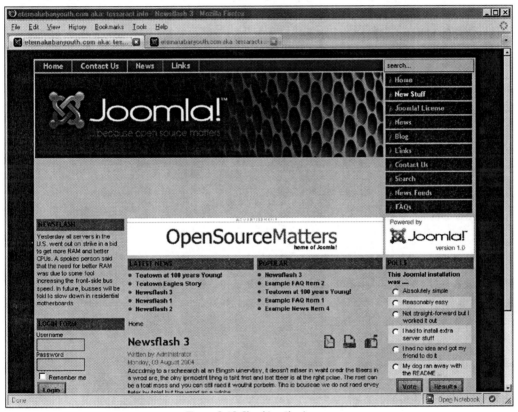

Figure 3.18 Checking the images

The final images that we need to add are, of course, in the main header. We'd also like the top navigation to be textured and lastly, we'd like our main background to have a gradient.

Top Navigation Images

Let's start with the top navigation. The textured background is actually just the subhead background. Locate the `#buttons_inner` rule and add a `background-image` property set to: `url(../images/subhead_bg.png)`.

Next, we want to put our faded background in. We want to ensure that the largest screen size can accommodate the gradient, so we've set it for a width of 4 pixels and a height of 1024 pixels.

Now surely many people will have screens much larger than this. That is why the main background color (`#070706`) is set to the bottommost color of the gradient. We will set our gradient to repeat from the top, left corner on the horizontal axis only and not to scroll. On screens larger than 1024 pixels high, the background color will stop, and the natural background color will pick up and go to infinity. This uses less bandwidth as we can use a smaller image instead of creating one that is much larger.

Locate the `body` rule and add the following values to the `background` property after the `background` color:

```
url(../images/main_bg.jpg) repeat-x fixed top left
```

The complete rule should now look like the following:

```
body {
    height: 100%;
    margin: 15px;
    margin-bottom: 1px;
    padding: 0px;
    font-family: Arial, Helvetica, Sans Serif;
    line-height: 120%;
    font-size: 11px;
    color: #333333;
    background: #070706 url(../images/main_bg.jpg) repeat-x fixed top
                                                              left;
}
```

Click **Save,** use *Alt+tab* to go over to your browser and **Refresh** to view your results.

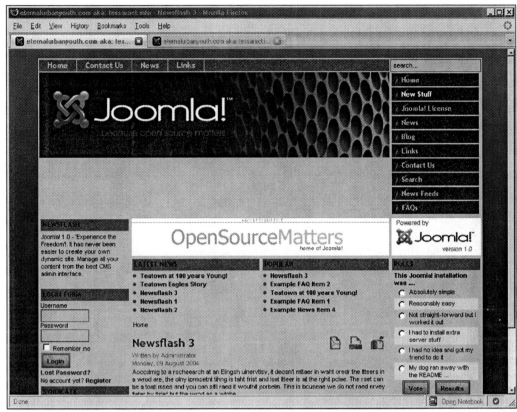

Figure 3.19 Checking the top navigation and background images

The Header Image

The background looks good. We last named our header `my_nature_header.jpg`. You probably noticed while working with the style sheet, that there were two header rules: `header_outer` and `header`. The `header` rule uses a `background` property with a `url` value. Let's replace the existing header image name with our header image name in that `url` property value. The rule should look like the following:

```
#header {
    float: left;
    padding: 0px;
    margin-right: 2px;
    width: 635px;
    height: 250px;
      background: url(../images/my_nature_header.jpg) no-repeat;
}
```

Click **Save,** use *Alt+tab* to go over to your browser, and **Refresh** to view your results.

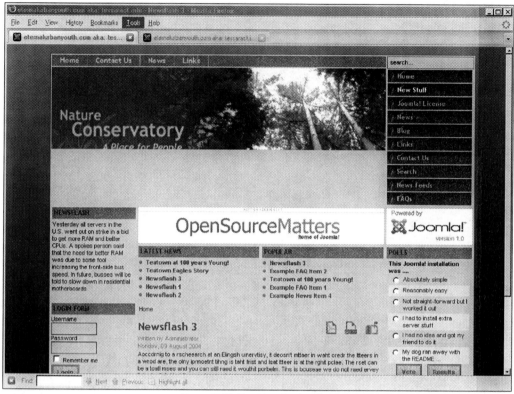

Figure 3.20 Checking the header

Well, it looks like we have just one last tweak to make. The `header` rule's `height` property is set to `150px`. Our header image was designed to match our main menu height, so let's change the `height` property to `250px`. Now, use *Alt+tab,* and **Refresh** to check your template.

Figure 3.21 Checking the header again

Congratulation! You now have your completed Joomla! template. If you'd like to compare your final `template_css.css` style sheet with the one that I came up with for this design, refer to the *Rhuk Redesign* section in the Appendix.

You will notice that we did all this without even touching the original template's XHTML in the `index.php` file! You will not always be so lucky. Let's now look at what's required to design your own XHTML layout from scratch.

The Truth about XHTML

We now have a working template of our design and that's great. Now, let's take it a step further.

You might have heard the word **semantic** used in conjunction with websites. A semantic site is simply a website whose presentation is completely separated from its content whose content is presented in a logical order of importance using only XHTML markup to define the type of content and data displayed.

This requires a structured organization of heading tags and the proper use of informational XHTML tags such as `label`, `address`, `cite`, and `dt` . This helps in informing browsers, other web applications, and code viewers what the content actually is.

A key distinction of a purely semantic site is the use of tables only to properly display tabular data and never to hold the layout of a web page together. The use of presentational HTML tags such as `bold` or `strong`, `italics` or `em`, etc. is eliminated because the layout and presentation of a semantic site are entirely controlled via the site's CSS file and never by any of its XHTML markup. Both, the site's XHTML markup and its CSS need to adhere to the web standards provided by the **W3C** (**World Wide Web Consortium**).

We've previously discussed in detail that this separation of content from layout is exactly what Joomla! does (and hence it's so hard to code with a WYSIWYG editor), but as you can see, there's a bit more to being semantic than just this separation. In the end, a Joomla! site is only as semantic and standard compliant as its template designer cares to make it.

While we would love to come up with a purely semantic, valid template, there are some limitations when working with Joomla! which prevent this. Most of these aren't really limitations when compared to the limitations placed on the features of Joomla! by the use of purely semantic requirements. So we'll make some reasonable compromises and apply consistent web standards to our template with a semantic-as-possible layout.

By having this as our goal, our Joomla! template will generally be less bandwidth intense, easier to maintain, accessible, and cross-compatible with as many current browsers as possible including new browsers, browsers that cater to users with disabilities as well as search engine bots, and some mobile formats.

Still pondering what semantic is? CSS Zen Garden is one of best examples of a semantic website in action: `http://csszengarden.com`. This site shows how the same semantic XHTML can be beautifully designed in dramatically different ways using CSS. The resulting pages look different, but all have the *exact* same core content. It's a great site to look through and you will probably find many inspiring designs and applications of CSS you never dreamed of.

Now that we've learned a little about semantic layout and we have a few goals for our newest Joomla! template, we're going to approximate the same visual design that we applied to the Rhuk template, but we're going to make sure that the content loads in a bit more semantically.

This means that the main content shows up before the sidebar information so that text readers, mobile devices, and search engine bots will understand our content better. We're also going to get as much module content as possible to output without tables. (We can't control some module content.) We will do all of this with a style sheet that's concise and easy to understand, and both our XHTML and CSS will validate to W3C web standards.

As a result of some of these self-imposed restrictions, our final visual design will be varied slightly from our table-based layout, but it will still be a great design. Let's get started!

New to XHTML, CSS, and Web Standards? AlistApart has an inspiring article: How to Grok Web Standards: `http://www.alistapart.com/articles/grokwebstandards`. `W3schools.com` has great tutorial references, which can introduce you to the exact ins and outs of XHTML and CSS (and just about anything else web-related!). Find out all about XHTML: `http://w3schools.com/xhtml/default.asp`. You can learn about the World Wide Web Consortium's standards, projects, and various validation tools here: `http://www.w3.org`.

Tabula Rasa

As before, you will need a development base. We are going to start off with a copy of our brand new template (because we're going to reuse a lot of the same images), give the directory a new name. Before we FTP it back, open up the `index.php` file and the `template_css.css` file. **Select All** and delete everything in both the files. Just do it! It will be OK.

Now, you will also want to open up that `templateDetails.xml` file and change the content in the `name` tag to something that you will recognize in your Joomla! Administration Panel.

If you're not working locally, FTP the directory into Joomla!'s template folder, and then *Alt+tab* over to your browser's Joomla! Administration Panel to ensure that the new template base is there.

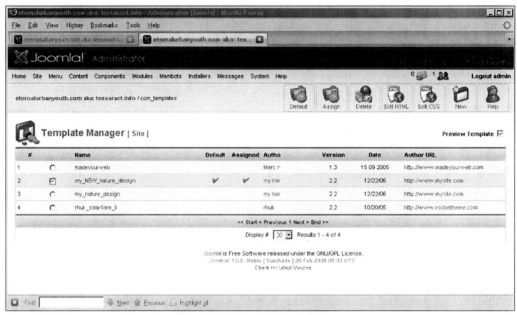

Figure 3.22 Your new template base

Set your new template as the *default, assigned to all pages*, as we did before with the other template and hit **Save**. You can test this by refreshing your template browser view where you should see *nothing*!

Figure 3.23 Your first template view

The DOCTYPE

In case you haven't been paying attention, we're going to be using XHTML, and for that, there are two common DOCTYPES: **Strict** and **Transitional**.

The Strict DOCTYPE is for the truly semantic, it means that you have absolutely no presentational markup in your XHTML. Every element in your XHTML merely aids in describing the type of text and data displayed and all your presentation styles come from your style sheet.

The Transitional DOCTYPE requires you to use the syntax of XHTML (with lower case tags and attribute names, all tags closed, including empty tags, and so on), but your template will not completely break if you reference a presentational HTML tag or other HTML 4.0 attributes in your markup.

Normally, we'd prefer the Strict DOCTYPE. However, at this time, it's hard to control everything that Joomla! outputs. (Some modules don't use heading tags for their titles, others output tables natively, and so on.) Also, there's the ultimate consideration when using Joomla! — the built-in WYSIWYG content editor.

Once your template is part of a working Joomla! site, the key feature that users are most likely going to be interested in leveraging is this WYSIWYG content editor. The use of the WYSIWYG editor to contribute content means that the site will be relying on basic HTML presentational tags (`strong`, `em`, `strike`, `u` tags, and the like) to format and display text.

As a result, we should not use the XHTML Strict DOCTYPE and instead rely on the XHTML Transitional DOCTYPE. This DOCTYPE will let us take advantage of HTML's presentational features within our XHTML.

About the TinyMCE WYSIWYG editor: Joomla! uses the TinyMCE WYSIWYG editor from Moxiecode Systems: `http://tinymce.moxiecode.com`. While this editor does display the CSS styles available to the template and it should be possible to block any tags that would be invalid to your DOCTYPE, keep in mind, that it would require some PHP back-end work in Joomla!. You'd also have to train the content contributors to understand what they can and can't do in the editor, including what CSS styles they should use to achieve certain kinds of formatting. The other option is to turn off the TinyMCE editor and force the contributors to use only plain text fields, entering semantic XHTML tags manually for their content. For the most part, this is exactly the kind of learning curve most organizations are trying to avoid. The promise of a visual editor that is reminiscent of their favorite word-processing program relieves that learning curve and is probably a big reason why they committed to using Joomla! in the first place. As a result, it's just better to use the XHTML Transitional DOCTYPE rather than limiting any of the key features of the Joomla! CMS for the sake of pure semantic markup.

Your DOCTYPE will be the *first* line of code in your `index.php` file and should look like this:

```
<!DOCTYPE html PUBLIC "-//W3C//DTD XHTML 1.0 Transitional//EN"
"http://www.w3.org/TR/xhtml1/DTD/xhtml1-transitional.dtd">
```

You should note, while being integral to a valid template, the DOCTYPE declaration itself is not a part of the XHTML document or an XHTML element. It does not use a closing tag, even though it does look a bit like an empty XHTML tag.

Attention Nvu and other WYSIWYG users: Chances are your WYSIWYG editor automatically placed a DOCTYPE and the required `html`, `header`, `title`, and `body` tags into your document when you opened your blank `index.php` file. That's great, but please go into your editor's preferences (**Tools | Preferences | Advanced** in Nvu) and make sure your **Markup** and **DTD** preferences are set to **XHTML** and **Transitional**. Nvu and possibly other editors will overwrite the DOCTYPE to whatever the preferences are set to if you switch between the **Normal** (a.k.a. **Design**) and **Source** (a.k.a. **Code**) views. Dreamweaver doesn't seem to have this problem, but you should set your DOCTYPE preferences there as well just to be safe.

The Main Body

After the DOCTYPE, we can add in the other essential requirements of XHTML Transitional markup which are as follows:

```
<html>
<head>
<title>My New Template Title</title>
</head>
<body> body parts go here </body>
</html>
```

You can hit **Save**, and then *Alt+tab* and hit **Refresh** to check it out in your browser.

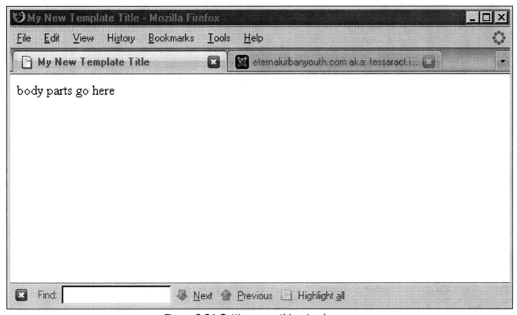

Figure 3.24 Getting something to show up

Getting the Layout Started

We are moving along in the right direction, but it's still not much to look at. So let's get the layout started. We'd like our template to have a standard header that stretches across all three columns. The middle column is the main content holder, and a footer running across the bottom of all three columns must fall beneath the longest extending column. Our basic layout will generally look something like the following:

Figure 3.25 Checking the fonts

Let's start off with some very basic XHTML code within the `index.php` files `body` tags. This will create the `div` tags for each segment: header, footer, side columns, and middle/main column:

```
<body>
<!--<a name="top"></a>-->
<div id="container"><!--container goes here-->
<div id="header">
header stuff goes here:
</div><!--//header-->

<!-- Begin #container2 this holds the content and sidebars-->
<div id="container2">

<!-- Begin #container3 keeps the left col and body positioned-->
<div id="container3">
<!-- Begin #content -->
<div id="content">
main content goes here
</div><!-- //content -->

<!-- #left sidebar -->
<div id="sidebarLT">
left side bar
</div><!--//sidebarLT  -->
</div><!--//container3-->

<!-- #right sidebar -->
<div id="sidebarRT">
right side bar (will include main menu)
</div><!--//sidebarRT -->
```

```
</div><!--//container2-->
<div id="top_navlist">
top nav will go here (css will place it up top)
</div><!--//top_navlist-->

<div id="footer">
footer information will go here
</div><!--//footer-->
</div><!--//container-->
</body>
```

Next, hit **Save**, use *Alt+tab* to get to your browser, and **Refresh** to view the following:

Figure 3.26 The semantic structure

Still not much to look at, but you can see our semantic goals at work. For instance, if a search engine bot or someone using a text-only browser or mobile device came and viewed our site, this is the semantic order they would see things in:

- **Header**: It's good to know whose stuff you're looking at.
- **Main content**: Here we can get right to the point of what we're looking for.
- **Left column content**: It is under the main content and should have the next most interesting items, news, login, and so on.

- **Right column content**: This would include the main menu. (It's best to push consistent navigation items down towards the bottom of the page so that they don't clutter up the content. Later on, we can make it easy for a text-only user to navigate down to that main menu with an anchor tag.)

- **Footer information**: As we've been scrolling down for so long, we have probably forgotten whose site we're on.

Moving navigation to the bottom: Some SEO experts believe another reason to semantically push the navigation items down the page as far as possible is that it encourages search engine bots to crawl and index more of the page before wandering off down the first link it comes to. The more content the bot can index at a time, the sooner you will be displayed on the search engine. Apparently, it can take months before a site is fully indexed, depending on its size. I have no idea if this is actually true, but its in line with my semantic structure based on usability, so no harm done. You will have to tell me if you think your content is getting better SE coverage based on this structure.

Let's now start to get this stuff looking like a website. You will notice each of our divs has an id name, and the divs that are going to be our three columns are wrapped inside an outer div called `container2`.

The main and left columns are wrapped in a div called `container3`. The entire set of divs including the `header` and `footer`, which are outside the `container2` div are wrapped in a main div called `container`.

This structure is going to hold our modules together and let them display semantically with the main content first, but the style will allow the left column to show up on the far left. This structure also ensures that the footer floats to the bottom of the longest column.

First, we will need to add a line of code to get our index page to associate with our CSS template and then be on our way. Place this code inside your `header` tags, under your `title` tags (starting at about line 7 in your `index.php` file):

```
<script type="text/javascript"> </script>
<style type="text/css" media="screen">

    @import url("<?php echo $mosConfig_live_site;?>
                 /templates/my_nature_design/css/template_css.css");

</style>
```

We're going to use the `@import` method to hide our style sheet from very old browsers such as Netscape 4. The empty JavaScript tag will keep our template from flickering unstyled content before loading in the style sheet.

Our basic CSS in the `template_css.css` file, which will position our XHTML `div` tags looks like the following:

```css
/* css */
/*////////// GENERAL //////////*/
    body {
       margin-top: 0px;
       margin-bottom: 30px;
       background-color: #FFFFFF;
    }

    #container {
       width: 850px;
       margin: 0 auto;
         margin-top: 20px;
       font-family: Verdana, Arial, Helvetica, sans-serif;
       font-size: 11px;
       color: #666666;
         background-color: #fff;
         border: 1px solid #333;
    }

    #container2 {
       width: 850px;
       margin: 0 auto;
       font-family: Verdana, Arial, Helvetica, sans-serif;
       font-size: 11px;
       line-height: 1.6em;
       color: #666666;
         border:1px solid #ff00cc;
    }

    #container3 {
       width: 635px;
         float: left;
       font-family: Verdana, Arial, Helvetica, sans-serif;
       font-size: 11px;
       line-height: 1.6em;
       color: #666666;
         border:1px solid #ff66cc;
      }

/*////////// HEADERS //////////*/
    #header {
       width: 850px;
         height: 140px;
       border: 1px solid #ff6600;
```

```
        padding-bottom: 10px;
        padding-top: 10px;
        clear: both;
    }
/*////////// CONTENT //////////*/
    #content {
        width: 400px;
        padding-left: 10px;
        padding-right: 10px;
        padding-top: 10px;
          border: 1px solid #006600;
          float: right;
      }
/*////////// NAV //////////*/
/*this is the tab layout*/

    #top_navlist {
        position: absolute;
        top: 20px;
      width:850px;
      line-height:normal;
        clear: both;
        border: 1px solid #006600;
      }
/*////////// RIGHT SIDEBAR //////////*/
    #sidebarRT {
        float: right;
        width: 175px;
        padding-left: 21px;
        padding-right: 10px;
        padding-top: 10px;
        border: 1px solid #000066;
      }
/*////////// LEFT SIDEBAR //////////*/
    #sidebarLT {
          float: left;
        width: 175px;
        padding-left: 21px;
        padding-right: 10px;
        padding-top: 10px;
          border: 1px solid #00ff66;
      }
/*////////// FOOTER //////////*/
```

```
#footer {
  margin-top: 15px;
  padding-top: 0px;
  padding-bottom:0px;
  clear: both;
  width: 850px;
  background-color:#FFF;
    border: 1px solid #ff0066;
}
```

By hitting **Save**, *Alt+tab*, and **Refresh**, the resulting CSS gives us a general layout template that looks like the following:

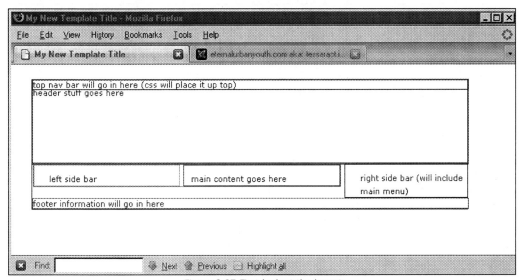

Figure 3.27 First look at the layout

Adding Joomla! Modules and Content

At last, we've got something that's starting to look like a website, and we're ready to start adding Joomla! template code.

First off, Joomla! needs a little information to ensure that everything is running properly, and we need to add this code *before* the DOCTYPE (right at line 1 of your `index.php` file):

```
<?php defined( '_VALID_MOS' ) or die( 'Direct Access to this location
                                      is not allowed.' ); ?>
```

This ensures that the template is being accessed via Joomla! itself (a.k.a. someone just normally hitting the website in the normal way) and that someone hasn't figured out the direct path to the template file and is trying to access it directly. If all is well, this code will do nothing (which is good because browsers, especially IE really hate it when you put something above the DOCTYPE). Otherwise, the viewer will simply see a **Direct Access to this location is not allowed** message.

Next, to keep in line with web standard requirements, let's modify our opening `html` tag with the following highlighted code, which will ensure that the language settings we chose in the Joomla! Administration Panel's **Global Configuration Settings** will be set in our template:

```
<html xmlns="http://www.w3.org/1999/xhtml" lang="<?php echo _LANGUAGE;
?>" xml:lang="<?php echo _LANGUAGE; ?>" >
```

Now, we're ready for our template's first meta-tag and to set up the header so that it will dynamically display our template's title in its self-generated `title` tag:

Place the highlighted code *inside* your `header` tag, *replacing* your existing `title` tag, which is just *before* your style sheet reference link tag:

```
<head>
<meta http-equiv="Content-Type" content="text/html;
                                        <?php echo _ISO; ?>" />
<?php
if ($my->id) { initEditor(); } ?>
<?php mosShowHead(); ?>
<script type="text/javascript"> </script>
<style type="text/css" media="screen">
    @import url("<?php echo $mosConfig_live_site;?> /templates/
                my_NEW_nature_design/css/template_css.css");
</style>
```

Again, after adding each chunk of code save your `index.php` file, and then press *Alt+tab* and **Refresh** to check the site in Firefox, even if you think there's not much to look at!

You should now see the browser's window displaying the title of your Joomla! site. If you right-click and **View Source** on the page, you'll see that the page is now generating a plethora of standard meta-tags with relevant keyword and description content based on what was paced into the CMS. (This example is based on the **View Source** for my template only, yours will be different.)

```
<title>eternalurbanyouth.com aka: tessaract.info - Newsflash
                                                    3</title>

<meta name="title" content="Newsflash 3" />
```

```
<meta name="author" content="Administrator" />
<meta name="description" content="Joomla - the dynamic portal engine
                                 and content management system" />
<meta name="keywords" content="Joomla, joomla" />
<meta name="Generator" content="Joomla! - Copyright (C) 2005 Open
                               Source Matters. All rights reserved." />
<meta name="robots" content="index, follow" />
<link rel="shortcut icon" />
```

We're now ready to add the actual content modules!

While reviewing our redesigned Rhuk template (a.k.a. my_nature_design), we noted the modules used in our site. After placing the module code in the index.php template, each module name gets wrapped in PHP code that looks like this:

```
<?php mosLoadModules ('module_name'); ?>
```

This means that the following mosLoadModules() codes need to be placed inside our div holders in our index.php template:

- `<?php mosLoadModules('user4'); ?>`
- `<?php mosLoadModules('left');?>`
- `<?php mosLoadModules('right');?>`
- `<?php mosLoadModules('top');?>`
- `<?php mosLoadModules('user1');?>`
- `<?php mosLoadModules('user2');?>`
- `<?php mosLoadModules('user3'); ?>`

The following list contains key content items are needed by our template; these are not modules and therefore, have their own special syntax:

- Displays the full name of the site:
  ```
  <?php echo $mosConfig_sitename; ?>
  ```
- Displays the breadcrumb trail:
  ```
  <?php mospathway() ?>
  ```
- Displays the actual body content:
  ```
  <?php mosMainBody(); ?>
  ```
- Displays the footer information:
  ```
  <?php include_once($mosConfig_absolute_path .'/includes/
  footer.php');?>
  ```

After placing each `mosLoadModules()` code and key content items into our template, our XHTML will now display information and content entered into the Joomla! CMS via the Joomla! Administration Panel. Your XHTML and PHP should look like this:

```
<body>

<div id="container"><!--container goes here-->

<div id="header">
header stuff goes here:
<?php echo $mosConfig_sitename; ?>
<?php mosLoadModules ( 'user4', -2 ); ?>
</div><!--//header-->

<!-- Begin #container2 this holds the content and sidebars-->
<div id="container2">

<!-- Begin #container3 keeps the left col and body positioned-->
<div id="container3">

<!-- Begin #content -->
<div id="content">
<?php mospathway() ?>
<?php mosMainBody(); ?>
</div><!-- //content -->

<!-- #left sidebar -->
<div id="sidebarLT">
left side bar:<br />
<?php mosLoadModules('left', -2);?>
<?php mosLoadModules('right', -2);?>
</div><!--//sidebarLT   -->

</div><!--//container3-->

<!-- #right sidebar -->
<div id="sidebarRT">
<?php mosLoadModules('top', -2);?>
<?php mosLoadModules('user1', -2);?>
<?php mosLoadModules('user2', -2);?>
</div><!--//sidebarRT -->

</div><!--//container2-->
```

```
<!--<a name="mainNav"> </a>-->
<div id="tabbar"> </div>

<div id="top_navlist">
<?php mosLoadModules ( 'user3', -2 ); ?>

</div>
<!--//top_navlist-->

<div id="footer">
<?php include_once($mosConfig_absolute_path .'/includes/footer.
php');?>
</div><!--//footer-->

</div><!--//container-->

</body>
```

When we save the index.php file, press *Alt+tab*, and click on **Refresh**, we get
something similar to the following:

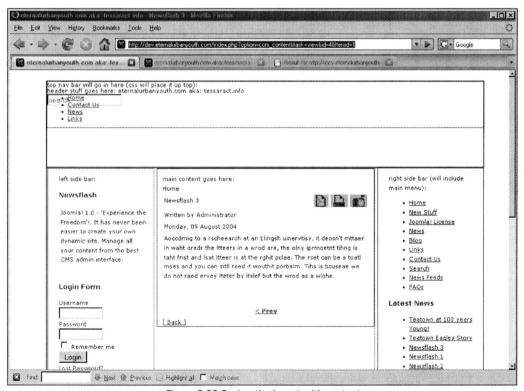

Figure 3.28 Seeing the layout with content

Module Options

You will notice that, in each bit of PHP code, in addition to the standard `mosLoadModule()` syntax that we discussed earlier, we've added a `, -2` after the module name. This has been done so that we can take advantage of the `$style` option in the `mosLoadModule()` functions.

You can set the `$style` option to be `0`, `1`, `-1`, `-2`, or `-3`. These settings provide you with the following options:

- `0`: Modules are displayed in a table with a single row and column. This is the default setting, and you will never really need to use it.
- `1`: Modules are displayed in a table with a multiple column rows, giving it the effect of being displayed *horizontally*, rather than *vertically* like the default.
- `-1`: Modules are displayed in plain-text output, without titles.
- `-2`: Modules are displayed wrapped in a single `<div>` tag, with titles in `<h3>` header tags.
- `-3`: Modules are displayed wrapped in several `<div>` tags with titles in `<h3>` header tags allowing for more complex CSS styling to be applied, such as stretchable, rounded corners.

We've chosen `-2` for our modules so that we can control their layout more easily with CSS and also reduce the number of tables in our template from over 19 to 8.

There is another way to control your menu module output. We want our menus to be displayed as bulleted lists or "flat lists" so that we can control them using more powerful CSS techniques.

Go to **Modules | Site Modules** and select **Main Menu**. You will then notice that in the Joomla! Administration Panel, you can select the menu's style. You can do this for all menus created with the **Module Manager** by selecting **Flat List** from the **Menu Style** option as shown in Figure 3.29:

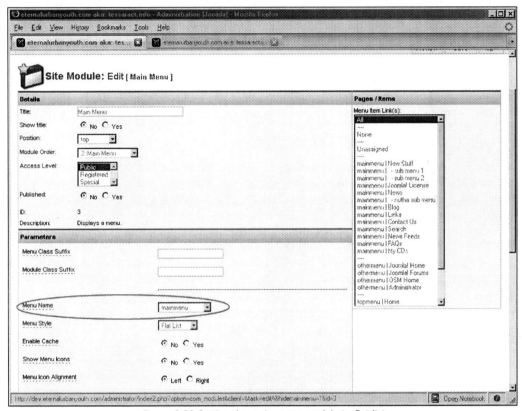

Figure 3.29 Setting the main menu module to flat list

Our **Top Menu, Latest News,** and **Popular** link menus are already using this **Flat List** option.

You've probably also noticed that, in restructuring the content semantically, the module names no longer match with the main div content holder areas. For instance, we have `mosLoadModules` code for both the **left** and **right** modules inside the left side div.

If you know that you're the only person who is going to be editing the template, this is probably fine. However, if you want to keep it clear and simple for your client or another Joomla! developer who might have to take over your template, then you will want to fix it. This can be done by going to your Joomla! Administration Panel, selecting **Modules | Site Modules**, and then repositioning the modules into more appropriately named position slots. You can also select **Site | Template Manager | Module Positions** and create your own custom module position names. You will then have to go back into the **Site Modules** manager and assign the elements to their new **Module Position**. Also, if you do change the names in the Joomla! Administration Panel, don't forget to update your template `index.php` file with the new module name inside the `mosLoadModules` code.

Be aware that, if you create your own position names, you will need to inform your client or Joomla! administrator that they need to create these module positions in the **Module Position Manager** in order for your template package to install properly and work.

Styling the New Template

We're now at a point very similar to where we started at the beginning of this chapter. We have a template which has its general layout in place. With a few key color changes, creative font application, and background images, we will pretty much have our well styled, new, and improved template.

Our CSS file already has our own core id rules for our template layout. We will start with assigning colors and general properties. After that, moving forward will be exactly like the Rhuk template (at the beginning of this chapter), we will select text and use Firefox's DOM inspector to show us what class and id rules the Joomla! content is spitting out so that we can create customized CSS rules for each element, bringing in our background images and final touches.

Awesome CSS List Techniques Listamatic and Listamatic2 from Max Design (`http://css.maxdesign.com.au/index.htm`) are wonderful resources for referencing and learning different techniques to creatively turn list items into robust navigation devices. It's what we've used to create our Top, Main, and Content Menus in our new semantic template. Our Top Menu uses the Rollover horizontal list nav bar: `http://css.maxdesign.com.au/listamatic/horizontal03.htm` and our Main Menu uses the Rollover lists: `http://css.maxdesign.com.au/listamatic/vertical08.htm`.

We just added our background images to these techniques and our navigation came right together.

Our header area has changed in size, so we will need to go back into our image editor and reexport a header image that's wider so that it accommodates our new semantic template better.

When all is said and done, and our fonts and images are placed into our `template_css.css` sheet, we should have a template that looks like the following:

Figure 3.30 Final Semantic Template View

To compare your template to mine, please refer to the *Table-less Design* section in Appendix A, where you can view the complete `template_css.css` style sheet and the `index.php` template code in its entirety.

If you felt accomplished earlier, then having reworked the `rhuk_solarflare_ii` template, you should be ecstatic at this point for accomplishing your first semantic, table-less, CSS Joomla! template. Great job!

Summary

You've now learned how to set up your development environment (a.k.a. sandbox) and an HTML editor for a smooth workflow. We also showed you some alternatives to a full Joomla! install. You now have two versions of your design—one with tables that was leveraged from the `rhuk_solarflare_ii` template and one from scratch, with semantic XHTML and CSS. Believe it or not, we're not quite done!

In the next chapter, we will continue working with our layouts, showing you some tips and tricks for debugging IE quirks as well as running it through a thorough validation process.

4
Debugging and Validation

For the sake of simplicity, I've made the process of debugging and validation a separate chapter. However, as you continue working and develop your own Joomla! templates, you will discover that life is much smoother if you debug and validate *at each step* of your template-development process. The full process will pretty much go like this: add some code; check to see if the page looks good in Firefox; check it in IE; make sure the page validates with W3C; if so, add next bit of code and repeat as necessary.

We're going to cover the basic techniques of debugging and validation that you should be employing throughout your development process. We'll dive into the W3C's XHTML and CSS validation services, look at using Firefox's JavaScript/Error console for robust debugging, and introduce you to the Firebug extension. I'll also give you a little troubleshooting insight as to some of the most common reasons due to which "good code goes bad", especially in IE and the various ways to remedy the problems.

Introduction to Debugging

Remember our initial work-flow chart in Chapter 3?

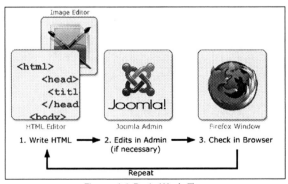

Figure 4.1 Basic Work Flow

I was insistent that your work flow be pretty much like this: edit -> check it -> then go back and edit some more. The main purpose of checking your template after adding each piece of code is of course to see if it looks OK and, if not, immediately *debug* that piece of code.

So your work flow really ends up looking something similar to the following:

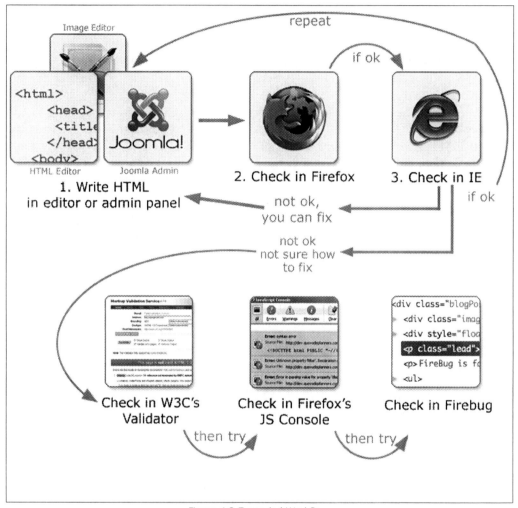

Figure 4.2 Expanded Workflow

You want to work with nice, small pieces or chunks of code. As soon as you see that something in your browser isn't looking right, you can check for validation and then fix it. The advantage of this workflow is that you know exactly what needs to be fixed and what code is to be blamed. You can ignore all the code that was looking fine and validating before. The recently added code is also the freshest in your mind so you're more likely to realize the solution needed to fix the problem.

If you add too many chunks of code before checking it in your browser and then discover something has gone awry, you'll have twice as much sleuthing to do in order to discover which bits of code are to be blamed. Again, your fail-safe is your backups.

You should be regularly saving backups of your template at good, stable stopping points. If you do discover that you just can't figure out where the issue is, rolling back to your last stable stopping point and starting over might be your best bet to getting back on track.

As mentioned in Chapter 3, you'll primarily design for Firefox and then apply any required fixes, hacks, and workarounds to IE. You'll do that for each piece of code you add to your template. As shown in Figure 4.1, first check your template in Firefox and if there's a problem, *fix it for Firefox first*. Then, check it in IE and make any adjustments for that browser.

At this point, you guessed it, more than half of the debugging process will depend directly on your own eyeballs and aesthetics. If it looks the way you intended it to look, works the way you intended it to work, check that the code validates and move on. When one of these *three* things doesn't happen (it doesn't look right, work right, or validate), you have to stop and figure out why.

Troubleshooting Basics

Suffice to say, it will usually be obvious when something is wrong with your template. The most common reasons for things being wrong are:

- Images are misnamed, mistargeted, or sized inappropriately.
- Markup text or PHP code that affects or breaks the **Document Object Model (DOM)** due to being inappropriately placed or having syntax errors in it.
- CSS rules that use incorrect syntax or conflict with later CSS rules.

The first point is pretty obvious when it happens. You see no images or worse, you might get those little ugly boxes marked with the x symbol in IE if they're called directly from the CMS. Fortunately, the solution is also obvious: you have to go in and make sure your images are named correctly if you're overwriting standard icons or images from another template. You also might need to go through your CSS file and make sure the relative paths to the images are correct.

For images that are not appearing correctly because they were sized inappropriately, you can go back to your image editor and fix them by re-exporting them, or you might be able to make adjustments in your CSS file to display a height and/or width that is more appropriate to the image you designed.

Don't forget about casing! Chances are you're developing your template with an installation of Joomla! on a local Windows machine with a server installed or a test server like RJS. But the actual Joomla! installation that your template is going to be installed into is more likely to be on a Linux web server. For some darn reason, Windows (even if you're running Apache, not IIS) will let you reference and call files with *only* the correct spelling required. Linux, in addition to spelling, requires the *casing* to be correct. You must be careful to duplicate *exact casing* when naming images that are going to be replaced and/or when referencing your own image names via CSS. Otherwise, it will look fine in your local testing environment, but you'll end up with a pretty ugly template when you upload it into your client's installation of Joomla! for the first time (which is just plain embarrassing).

For the latter two points, one of the best ways to debug syntax errors that cause visual "wonks" is not to have syntax errors in the first place. (Don't roll your eyes just yet.)

This is why, in Figure 4.2, we advocate you to *not only* visually check your design as it progresses in Firefox and IE, but also test for *validation*.

I understand it's easy to add some code, run a visual check in Firefox and IE, see everything looks OK, and then flip right back to your HTML editor to add more code. Hey, "time is money" and you'll just save that validation part until the very end. After all, that's just "icing on the cake", right?

The problem with debugging purely based on the visual output is, all browsers (some more grievously than others) will try their best to help you and properly interpret less than ideal markup. One piece of invalid markup might very well look OK initially, until you add more markups and then the browser can't interpret your intentions between the two types of markup anymore. The browser will pick its own best option and display something guaranteed to be ugly.

You'll then go back and play around with the last bit of code you added (because everything was fine until you added that last bit, so that must be the offending code) which may or may not fix the problem. The next bits of code might create other problems and what's worse is you'll recognize a code chunk that you know should be valid! You're then frustrated, scratching your head as to why the last bit of code you added is making your template "wonky" when you know, without a doubt, it's perfectly fine code!

The worst case scenario seen in this type of visual-only debugging is that template developers get desperate, and randomly start making all sorts of odd hacks and tweaks to their markup and CSS to make it look right.

Miraculously, they often manage to make it look right, but in only *one* browser. Most likely, they've inadvertently discovered what the first invalid syntax was and unwittingly applied it across *all* the rest of their markup and CSS. Thus, one browser started consistently interpreting the *bad* syntax! The template designer is then convinced that the other browser isn't good, and designing these non-WYSIWYG, dynamic templates is quite problematic.

Avoid all that frustration. Even if it looks great in both browsers, run the code through the W3C's XHTML and CSS validators. If something turns up invalid, no matter how small or pedantic the validator's suggestion might be (and they do seem pedantic at times), incorporate the suggested fix into your markup now, before you continue working. This will keep any small syntax errors from compounding future bits of markup and code into big visual "uglies" that are hard to track down and trouble shoot.

Last, your CSS file might get fairly big, fairly quickly. It's easy to forget that you have already created a rule and accidentally create another rule of the same name. It's all about cascading, so whatever comes later overwrites what came first.

Double rules: You'll remember that we ran into this issue with the original rhuk template in Chapter 3. The author had two body rules, and we had to troubleshoot this before we could get the background color changed. It's an easy mistake to make, but validating using W3C's CSS validator will point this out right away. However, this is not the case for double properties within rules! W3C's CSS validator will not point out double properties if both properties use correct syntax. This is one of the reasons why the !important hack returns valid.

Perhaps you found a site that has a nice CSS style or effect that you like and so you copied those rules into your template's CSS. It's easy to introduce errors by wrongly copying in bits of code. A small syntax error in a property towards the bottom of a rule may seem OK at first, but might cause problems with properties added to the rule later. This can also affect the entire rule or even the rule after it. Also, if you're copying CSS, be aware that older sites might be using depreciated CSS properties, which might be technically OK if they're using an older HTML DOCTYPE, but won't be OK for the XHTML DOCTYPE you're using.

Again, validating your markup and CSS as you're developing will alert you to syntax errors, depreciated properties, and duplicate rules which could compound and cause issues in your style sheet down the line.

Advanced Troubleshooting

Take some time to understand the XHTML hierarchy. You'll start running into validation errors and CSS styling issues if you wrap a "normal" element inside an "in-line" only element such as putting a `header` tag inside an `anchor` tag (`<a href`, `<a name`, and so on) or wrapping a `div` tag inside a `span` tag.

Avoid triggering quirks mode in IE. This, if nothing else, is one of the most important reasons for using the W3C HTML validator. There's no real way to tell if IE is running in quirks mode. It doesn't seem to output that information anywhere (that I've found). However, if any part of your page or CSS isn't validating, it's a good way to trigger quirks mode in IE.

The first way to avoid quirks mode is to make sure your DOCTYPE is valid and correct. If IE doesn't recognize the DOCTYPE or if you have huge conflicts like an XHTML DOCTYPE, and you use all-cap HTML 4.0 tags in your markup, IE defaults into quirks mode and from there on who knows what you'll get in IE.

My template stopped centering in IE! The most obvious thing that happens when IE goes into quirks mode is that IE will stop centering your layout in the window properly if your CSS is using the: **margin: 0, auto;** technique. If this happens, immediately fix all validation errors in your page. Another obvious item is to note if your `div` layers with borders and padding are sized differently between browsers. If IE is running in quirks mode it will incorrectly render the box model, which is quite noticeable if you're using borders and padding in your divs.

Another item to keep track of is to make sure you don't have anything that will generate any text or code above your DOCTYPE. The only item that should be placed above that item in your template is the `<?php defined( '_VALID_MOS' )` or `die( 'Direct Access to this location is not allowed.' ); ?>` code we discussed in Chapter 3.

Firefox will read your page until it hits a valid DOCTYPE and then proceed from there, but IE will break and go into quirks mode.

Fixing CSS across Browsers

If you've been following our debug->validate method described earlier, then for all intents and purposes, your layout should look pretty spot-on between both browsers.

In the event that there is a visual discrepancy between Firefox and IE, in most cases it's a box-model issue arising because you're running in quirks mode in IE. Generally, box-model hacks apply to pre-IE-6 browsers: IE 5.x and apply to IE 6 if it's running in quirks mode. Again, running in quirks mode is to be preferably avoided, thus eliminating most of these issues.

If your markup and CSS are validating (which means you shouldn't be triggering quirks mode in IE but we've had people "swear" to us that their page validated yet quirks mode was being activated), you might "live with it" rather than trying to sleuth what's causing quirks mode to activate.

Basically, IE 5.x and IE 6 quirks mode, don't properly interpret the box-model standard, and thus "smush" your borders and padding inside your box's width instead of adding to the width as the W3C standard recommends. However, IE does properly add margins! This means that, if you've got a div set to 50 pixels wide, with a 5 pixel border, 5 pixels of padding, and 10px of margin, in Firefox your `div` is actually going to be 60 pixels wide with 10 pixels of margin around it, taking up a total of 70 pixels of space.

In quirks mode IE, your box is kept at 50px wide (so that it's probably taller than your Firefox `div` because the text inside is wrapping at 40 pixels), yet it does have 10 pixels of margin around it. You can quickly see how even a one pixel border, some padding, and a margin can start to make a big difference in layout between IE and Firefox!

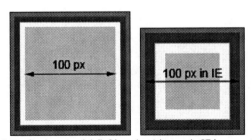

Figure 4.3 Firefox box model (left) and quirks mode IE box model (right)

Almost everyone is now using IE 6 (and probably 7), and we find that as long as we stay in strict mode and not fall into quirks mode, we don't have too many issues with box-model rendering. Occasionally, we still notice that relative (% or .em) values render a little differently for our properties, but that's not box model, so much as what the two browsers consider, say, 20% to be in pixels. Even so, as long as your layout doesn't look weird, it's generally OK if you're template's container divs are a hair wider in one browser over the other. If you're using relative values to measure everything out, your placement will stay intact.

If for some reason you feel you know what you're getting into and have intentionally used markup syntax that's triggering quirks mode in IE (or you just can't figure out why or maybe your client insists on designing for IE 5.x for Windows), then it's time for some hacks.

The cleanest hack is the !important, hack, which we briefly reviewed in Chapter 3 when the original rhuk designer used it in his CSS. We like it because it lets our CSS still render as valid. However, you should note that the !important value is valid syntax and meant to be used as an accessibility feature of CSS. It's not a value that was ever meant to affect design. The fact is that IE does not recognize it is a bug and though it's very simple and easy to implement, it is not recommended to be used liberally as a design fix. The understanding is that eventually IE will fix this bug so that it adheres to accessibility standards and then your hack will no longer work (especially if IE doesn't change anything about how it runs in quirks mode). The thing is, all hacks rely on exploiting various bugs in IE to some extent, and may or may not continue to work with future service patches and upgrades to IE.

To implement the !important hack, take the width, height, margin, or padding property that has the discrepancy in it and double it. Place the value that looks best in Firefox *first* and add the !important value after it. Then, place the value in the duplicate property that looks best in IE *below* the first property. You should have something that looks like the following:

```
.classRule{
    height: 100px !important;
    height: 98px;
}
```

Firefox and all other browsers will read the value with the !important value after it as though it were the last value in the rule. IE ignores the !important value and thus regular old cascading kicks in, so it reads the actual last property value in the rule.

Other IE hacks include using the * star selector bug hack and the _ underscore hack. Both hacks work on the same general principle as the !important hack, that IE does or doesn't recognize; something that all the other browsers do or don't recognize themselves. You can find out more about the underscore hack from WellStyled. com: http://wellstyled.com/css-underscore-hack.html. A good overview of the star selector bug can be found here: http://www.info.com.ph/~etan/w3pantheon/style/starhtmlbug.html.

Be aware that these two hacks will show up as validation errors in your CSS. Plus, the star and underscore hacks are rumored to no longer be viable in IE7. At this time, we're still using IE6 and you must chose to use these three hacks at your discretion.

Out-of-the-Box-Model Thinking

Your best bet is again, not to use hacks and create alternatives to using a box-model hack. This can be achieved in a couple of ways. A good one is to break your XHTML markup down a little more so that it's in more controllable chucks. For instance, instead of one div layer:

```
<div id="leftSide">...</div>
```

This div layer has the following assigned rule:

```
#leftSide{
width: 200px;
border: 2px;
padding: 10px;
}
```

This is clearly going to give you problems in quirks mode IE, because the div will stay at 200 pixels wide and "smush" your border and padding inside it, it would be better to tuck an extra div or other XHTML element inside the leftSide id as follows:

```
<div id="leftSide"><div>...</div></div>
```

Then, you can control the width and borders much more accurately using CSS that looks like the following:

```
#leftSide{
width: 200px;
}
#leftSide div{
border: 2px;
padding: 10px;
}
```

By using a fix like this, your div will always be 200 pixels wide, despite the border and padding, in *all* browsers, regardless of quirks mode. Plus, your XHTML markup and CSS stays valid.

Container divs: We find working with CSS and XHTML markup in this way also keeps you from getting into other trouble. Let's say we "do the math" to figure our column widths and margins out, but then either forget to account for borders and padding in our design or maybe just decide to add them later. In browsers like Firefox, a miscalculation or late addition like that will throw our columns off, especially if their containing div is set to an exact width. This results in ugly, stacked columns. We like to use clean containing divs to only control our placement, width, and margins. Then, we let inner divs (which will by default, expand to the width of the containing div) take on borders, padding, and other visual stylings. This is a good way to get your math right and keep it right, no matter what design additions may come later.

You can set your own main container divs in your template and then load in your Joomla! modules using the -2 property in your `mosLoadModules` PHP Code. This will let you control exact placement with your own divs and then style the internal Joomla! output divs. You can have even more divs to work with in your Joomla output if you use the -3 property as specified in Chapter 3.

Your final alternative is to just create two uh-hacked style sheets for your template and let each browser call them in.

This isn't as bad as it seems. The bulk of your CSS can stay in your main CSS file. You can then call this specific IE style sheet code below which will load additionally only if the browser is IE.

In the IE style sheet, you'll duplicate the rules and correct the properties that were not looking correct in Firefox. Because this style sheet will load underneath your main style sheet, any duplicated rules will overwrite the original rules in your first style sheet. The result is CSS styling that's perfect in Firefox and IE. However, if you run the CSS validator in IE, it will alert you of the double rules.

In your `index.php` template, add this code after your full style sheet call:

```
<!--[if IE]>
    <link rel="stylesheet" type="text/css" href="ie-fix.css"
      media="screen, projection" />
<![endif]-->
```

Is that a conditional comment?

Yes it is. In the past, your best bet to load in the proper style sheet would have been using a server-side script to detect the browser with something like PHP. You could use a JavaScript as well, but if someone had JavaScript disabled in their browser, it wouldn't work. Not everyone can be a PHP whiz, hence, we advocate the method above for loading in your two style sheets with minimal hassle. The above method is also the best for keeping your two style sheets as simple as possible (having a main one, then one with IE fixes). However, you can apply all sorts of control to the conditional comment above, giving you quite a bit of power in how you dole out your CSS. For instance, you can specify what version of IE to check for IE 5, IE 6, or IE 7, you can also inverse the condition and only load in the CSS if the browser is not IE, by placing another ! exclamation point in front of the IE, for example: `<![if !IE]> ...<![endif]>`. Learn all about this conditional CSS tag at `http://www.quirksmode.org/css/condcom.html`.

You have to add that code in the template `index.php` file. We would prefer something like this could be implemented in the actual CSS file and then only parts of our CSS would need to be specific and we'd only need to keep track of one file. But alas, you have to add it to your template's `index.php` file.

Also, please note that we advocate using the `@import` method for bringing in style sheets but that method will not work within the `<![if IE]>` CSS check. Use the standard link import tags used above.

CSS trouble-shooting technique: The best way to quickly get a handle on a rule that's gone awry is to set a border and general background color to it. You'll notice we did this to our initial layout in Chapter 3. Make the color something obvious and not part of your color scheme. Often times, using this technique will reveal quite unexpected results, like showing that a div was inadvertently set somehow to just 500 wide instead of 500px wide or perhaps that another `div` is pushing against it in a way we didn't realize. It will quickly bring to your attention all the actual issues affecting your object's box model that need to be fixed to get your layout back in line. Using Firebug? Firebug will outline your CSS-defined elements for you. Read on to find out more about this great Firefox extension.

The Road to Validation

You'll want to always validate your XHTML first. This is just as well since W3C's CSS validator won't even look at your CSS if your XHTML isn't valid.

Go to `http://validator.w3.org/`, and if your file is on a server, you can just enter in the URL address. If you're working locally from your browser, you'll need to **Save Page As**, and save an HTML file of your template with Joomla! output and upload that full output to the validator using the upload field provided.

Ideally, when you run your XHTML through the validator, you'll get a screen with a green bar that says **This Page Is Valid XHTML 1.0 Transitional!**

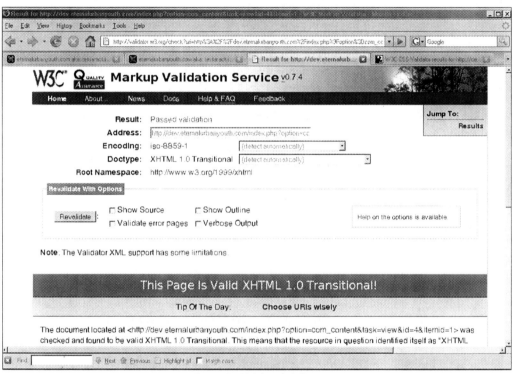

Figure 4.4 Validated XHTML

You can then move on to checking your CSS. Open up another tab in your browser and go to `http://jigsaw.w3.org/css-validator/`. Again, same deal. If you're working off a server, then just enter the address of your CSS file on the development site and check the results. Otherwise, you'll have to use the **by File Upload** tab and upload a copy of your CSS file.

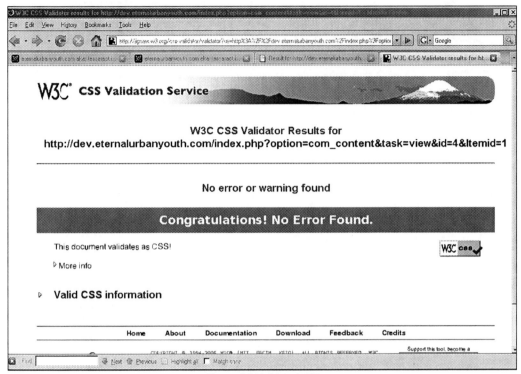

Figure 4.5 Validated CSS

Here you'll want to see another screen with a green bar that says **Congratulations! No Error Found.**

Figure 4.6 Errors found in XHTML

If you entered or uploaded your XHTML and you didn't get a screen with a green bar, you'll have to scroll down below the red bar and take a look at what errors were reported.

In our example, you can see that we have a typo in one of our divs (looks like an odd **s** got in there somehow) and we have an image tag that doesn't have the proper closing **/** in it. Wherever possible, you'll note that the validator tries to tell us how to fix the error. Whenever a recommendation is made, go ahead and implement it.

We'll need to fix these two errors and run the validation again to make sure we're now validating. Don't just think you can fix the errors listed and move on without validating again. Occasionally, an error will be so grave that it will block other errors from being picked up until it's fixed. Always validate -> fix -> validate, until you get that green bar telling you that you're good to move on.

Where's My Error? The validator tells us which line the offensding code appears in, which is why we love HTML editors that display the line number to the left in our **Code** view. However, once your template is pulling in content from the CMS, the offending line of code is not necessarily the same code line in your template anymore. So where's the error? We work around this by copying some *unique* text from the error, in our case **s>**. You can also use text from an `alt` or `id` tag within the reported object. Then use the **Find** option in your editor to directly locate the error.

Once your XHTML validates, you can move on to checking your CSS.

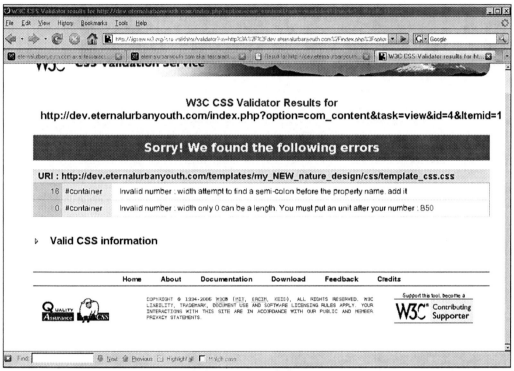

Figure 4.7 Errors found in CSS

If you don't get the green bar, the validator will display the offending error and again offer suggestions on how to fix it. The CSS validator will also show you the offending code line. This is handy as your style sheet is not affected by the Joomla! CMS output so you can go right to the line mentioned and make the suggested fix.

Advanced Validation

Perhaps you've discovered (because you are talented indeed and would find something like this) that your XHTML and CSS validate, yet somehow something is still wrong with your layout. Or maybe, you're using some special JavaScripts to handle certain aspects or features of your template. W3C's XHTML and CSS tools won't validate JavaScript. If you find yourself in this situation you will have to dig a little deeper to get to the root of the problem or make sure all aspects (like JavaScripts) of your template are valid.

Firefox's JavaScript/Error Console

You can use Firefox's JavaScript/Error Console (called the JavaScript Console in 1.x and Error Console in 2.x) to debug and validate any JavaScripts your template is using. Go to **Tools | Error Console** in your browser to activate it. You can also activate it by typing **javascript:** into your address bar and hitting *Enter* on your keyboard.

Figure 4.8 Errors found in Console

You will be pleasantly surprised to find out that the console will also spit out several warnings and errors for CSS rules that the W3C's validators probably didn't tell you about. The **Error Console** does hold a log of all errors it encounters for all pages you've looked at. Therefore, the best way to proceed with the **Error Console** is to first hit **Clear**, and then reload your page to be sure you're only looking at current bugs and issues for that specific page.

Again, the **Error Console** will let you know what file and line the offending code is in so that you can go right to it and make the suggested fix.

Firebug

A more robust tool is Joe Hewitt's Firebug extension for Firefox at
`http://www.getfirebug.com/`.

This extension will find them all: XHTML, CSS, JavaScript, and even little weird
tid-bit things happening to your **DOM (Document Object Model)** on the fly. There
are a variety of fun inspectors, and just about all of them are invaluable.

Once you have Firebug installed into your browser, you can turn it off and on by
hitting *F12* or going to **View | Firebug**.

Our favorite is the options available for CSS. Firebug will show you your box
models with different colored shading and let you see the measurements of each
edge. Moreover, the latest version of Firebug lets you make edits on the fly to easily
experiment with different fixes before committing them to your actual document.

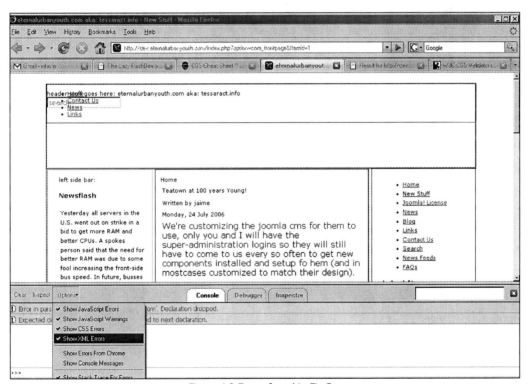

Figure 4.9 Errors found in FireBug

DOM: We've mentioned the DOM a few times in this book, learning about the Document Object Model can really enhance your understanding of your XHTML templates (or any web page you design) as well as help you in having a better understanding of how to effectively structure your CSS rules and write cleaner, accurate JavaScripts. Find out more from the W3Schools at `http://w3schools.com/htmldom/default.asp`.

Extra Credit

If you want a better understanding of how all-text browsers or users on mobile devices are viewing your site, you can use Google's mobile viewing tool to give you an idea. This may help you visualize how to better arrange your site semantically for users in these categories.

You'll now be able to see how your complete site looks without CSS styling, and you can even turn off images. Use this if you think that your Joomla! content is loading in logically and in the order of importance you prefer for your viewers (that is semantically). Also keep in mind this is very similar to how a search engine bot will crawl your page from top to bottom, and thus the order in which the content will be indexed.

Summary

In this chapter we reviewed the basic wash -> rinse -> repeat process to debugging and validating your template's code. You learned how to use the W3C's XHTML and CSS validation tools and we further explored the value of using Firefox as a valuable development tool using its JavaScript Console and Firebug extension.

Next, it's time to package up your design and send it to your client. Get ready to look at some XML.

5
Your Template in Action

Now that we've got our template designed, styled, and looking great, we just have one last thing to do. It's time to share your template with your client, friends, or the rest of the world.

We'll discuss how to set up your `templateDetails.xml` file and we'll go over what each part of that file does in detail. We'll then discuss compressing your template files into the ZIP file format and running some test installations of your template package in the Joomla! Administration Panel. We'll even go over a few troubleshooting options if, for some reason, your template doesn't install correctly.

A Picture's Worth

Before we begin wrapping up our template package, we'll need one more thing: the template's preview thumbnail. Take a screenshot of your final layout and save it to be about 200 to 205 pixels wide. Place your image in your template's root directory structure so that it's next to your `templateDetails.xml` file. The thumbnail file must be named `template_thumbnail.png`. Later, we'll assign this image to tag the `templateDetails.xml` file.

If all goes well, when we test install our package, our Joomla! Administration Panel should give us a rollover sample of the template design.

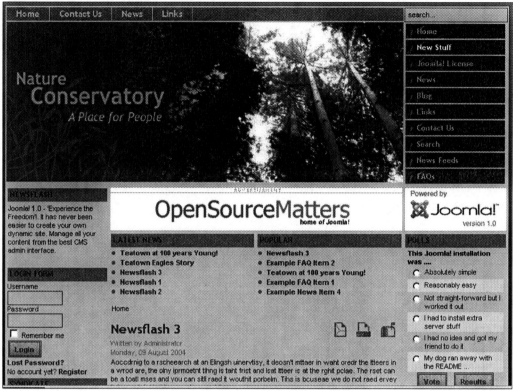

Figure 5.1 My_Nature_Web template preview.

Easy XML

The first thing we need to do so as to pull our template together is to put all the required file information into our `templateDetails.xml` file. You can leave behind any preconceptions that XML documents are incredibly complicated things that only the super geeky, non-visual designers traverse. You'll recall we already looked at this file in Chapter 3 and it wasn't scary at all.

This XML document is extremely simple, but nonetheless you'll want to be careful with the syntax in it. An accidentally deleted > bracket or forgetting a closing `</nodeName>` tag will break the XML file, and your final ZIP file will not upload and install properly. With a little understanding of what each tag does and some attention to detail, you shouldn't have any problems.

Most good HTML editors like Dreamweaver will open up your XML document and keep it intact and valid. You can use an XML document editor like Altova's XML Spy `http://www.altova.com/`, but this software is prohibitively expensive, especially if you don't intend on become an XML architect. If you're editing on a Windows PC, then XML Marker from SymbolClick `http://symbolclick.com/` is a good free editor. An XML editor will usually let you view the XML's structure in a *grid* format, and let you edit node content and attributes easily without disturbing the surrounding syntax.

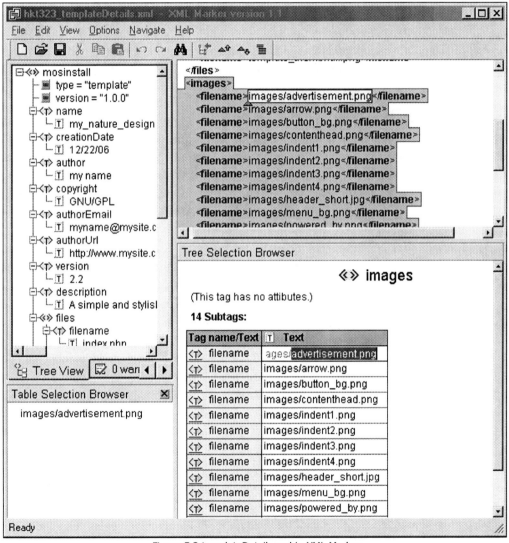

Figure 5.2 templateDetails.xml in XML Marker

There are also component extensions for Joomla! that you can use to generate your `templateDetails.xml` file. Yes, this is a bit confusing and sounds like the horse before the cart. As you can see we've been developing our Joomla! templates by hand—from scratch by uploading a base template folder and modifying the files. The following extensions will allow you to generate your `templateDetails.xml` file from Joomla!, once you've completed your template design. I have not used these extensions myself, but if you're really uncomfortable working with XML these might be a good option for you.

There's the Template XML generator component: `http://extensions.joomla.org/component/option,com_mtree/task,viewlink/link_id,355/Itemid,35/`

And the Joomla! TemplateDetails.xml Generator: `http://extensions.joomla.org/component/option,com_mtree/task,viewlink/link_id,585/Itemid,35/`

Getting to Know Your XML

Whether or not you'll be working with an XML generator component, your HTML editor, or an XML editor, it's good to understand what the `templateDetails.xml` file contains and what each part of it is meant to do. If there are any issues with your package, knowing what each part does will greatly ease troubleshooting and aid in fixing your installation. If any piece of your template is not added to this file in the appropriate tags, your package will produce errors upon installation.

Here's our `templateDetails.xml` file as it stands as of Chapter 3:

```
<?xml version="1.0" encoding="iso-8859-1"?>
<mosinstall type="template" version="1.0.0">
    <name>my_nature_design</name>
    <creationDate>12/22/06</creationDate>
    <author>my name</author>
    <copyright>GNU/GPL</copyright>
    <authorEmail>myname@mysite.com</authorEmail>
    <authorUrl>http://www.mysite.com</authorUrl>
    <version>2.2</version>
    <description>A simple and stylish template. Based on Rhuk's
                          Solarflare II design</description>
    <files>
        <filename>index.php</filename>
        <filename>template_thumbnail.png</filename>
    </files>
    <images>
        <filename>images/advertisement.png</filename>
        <filename>images/arrow.png</filename>
```

```
            <filename>images/button_bg.png</filename>
            <filename>images/contenthead.png</filename>
            <filename>images/indent1.png</filename>
            <filename>images/indent2.png</filename>
            <filename>images/indent3.png</filename>
            <filename>images/indent4.png</filename>
            <filename>images/header_short.jpg</filename>
            <filename>images/menu_bg.png</filename>
            <filename>images/powered_by.png</filename>
            <filename>images/spacer.png</filename>
            <filename>images/subhead_bg.png</filename>
            <filename>images/title_back.png</filename>
        </images>
        <css>
            <filename>css/template_css.css</filename>
        </css>
    </mosinstall>
```

Now, all we really changed was the name of the template so that we could differentiate it from the original Rhuk template in our Joomla! Administration Panel. The rest of the information in this XML file is still Rhuk's. Let's learn what each tag does.

```
<?xml version="1.0" encoding="iso-8859-1"?>
```

This is XML's DOCTYPE, and you're pretty much going to leave it alone. We're pretty sure that our template is only going to be used primarily with computers using Western languages, so we'll leave the encoding as iso-8859-1. If you're hoping for a wide distribution of your template on machines using other languages, it might be better to set this to UTF-8.

```
<mosinstall type="template" version="1.0.0">
```

You'll notice that everything else is tucked into this <mosinstall... tag. Don't forget to *add* the closing </mosinstall> tag at the very end of your file!

The attributes type="template" and version="1.0.0" tell the installer that we are installing a template and also what version of Joomla! it's optimally designed for. If you're using a development version of Joomla! that's greater than 1.0.0 (probably 1.0.8 or 1.0.12 as at the time of writing) you should enter those numbers into the version attribute. We'll change the version number 1.0.8 for our templateDetails.xml file.

```
<name>my_nature_design</name>
```

As mentioned, we added our own template name in Chapter 3 when we set up our development area. This tag defines the name of your template. This name is also used to generate the directory within the template directory. As a result, you cannot use characters that the file system cannot handle, like spaces or special symbols. You'll notice in Chapter 3 that the file directory that we manually created and copied was named with the same name as the one we entered into the `<name>` tag. This is required for the template to work properly.

```
<creationDate>12/22/06</creationDate>
```

We did update this initially as well. Obviously, you'll enter the date when your template was created. While the double-digit `month/day/year` format is standard, there are no real requirements for this tag. You can use any date format you'd like such as a general "May 2007", the more American "May 30, 2007", or "2007-05-30". Just pick something you know your template's users are going to recognize as a date.

```
<author>my name</author>
```

Here you'll add your name to the template, or perhaps a team, group, or corporate name if a group of you designed the template together.

```
<copyright>GNU/GPL</copyright>
```

You'll place your copyright information in this tag. Rhuk released the `solar_flare_ii` template under the GNU/GPL license. If you're not familiar with the GNU/GPL License you can learn more about it at `http://www.gnu.org/copyleft/gpl.html`. You may wish to do the same with your template. If you do this, it has to be freely distributed, available to all, and changeable by all with no permissions necessary so long as they acknowledge you.

If you've created a completely original design that you intend to sell commercially, or just want to be able to grant permission for any other possible use, you'll need to place specific copyright information and the name of the person or organization that holds the copyright. Something like © **2007 My Name, All Rights Reserved**, is generally recognized as legal with or without any formal copyright filing procedures (but you should look up how to best formally copyright your design material).

Our design is leveraged from the Rhuk design for educational purposes, although the GNU/GPL license is more than adequate. Its text is perhaps a bit "software-ish"and "tech-heavy" for our intended audience, so we're going to redistribute the new nature template under the more general-public-friendly Creative Commons License. We'll use the CC Labs DHTML License Chooser to assist us in selecting an appropriate license. It can be found at `http://labs.creativecommons.org/dhtmllicense/`:

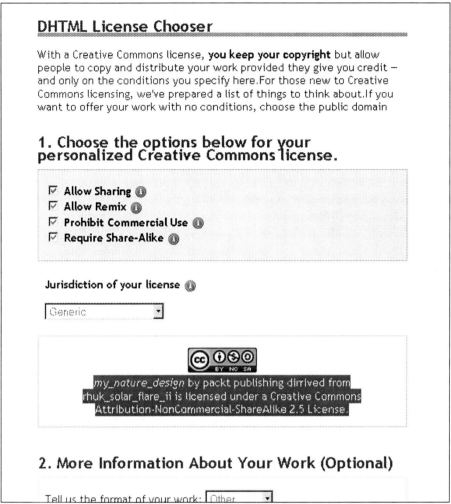

Figure 5.3 Creative Commons DHTML license chooser

We'll of course allow sharing of the template, and let others "remix" and derive new works from it (as we remixed Rhuk's) with proper credit. We will, however, prevent it from being used commercially, and use the **Require Share-Alike** option. This means that no one can legally take the template package and offer it for sale or use it in such a way that it generates income for them without our permission. If they reuse or redesign the package in any other non-commercial way they're free to do so, they're simply required to give us and Rhuk due credit.

Our licensing agreement looks like the following:

my_nature_design by Tessa Blakeley Silver for Packt Publishing, remix inspired by: rhuk_solar_flare_ii, is licensed under a Creative CommonsAttribution-NonCommercial-ShareAlike 2.5 License.

The end result is a license that keeps the spirit of the GNU/GPL license but is much less vague. It tells the user upfront that it allows sharing which is important to us for educational purposes, gives continued credit to the original Rhuk author, prevents commercial distribution without permission, and by requiring share-alike encourages a continued friendly Joomla!-esque atmosphere for open-source collaboration. It also states the version number of the license making it very easy for anyone to look it up and read it in detail.

Additionally, a **Licensing Primer for Developers and Designers** can be found on the Joomla! forums at `http://forum.joomla.org/index.php/topic,22653.0.html`.

```
<authorEmail>myname@mysite.com</authorEmail>
<authorUrl>http://www.mysite.com</authorUrl>
```

Here, we'll place a good contact email address for people who might have questions about the template. This is especially important if you're going to use a straight-up copyright. Make sure people who are seeking permission to use your design can do so, there's probably cash at stake! While publishing via a Copyright, GPL, or CC license, it's a good idea to ensure that the email address is best suited for taking technical questions about your template. You are not responsible to be available for "tech-support", especially under the GNU/GPL or CC license, as everyone's system and use of Joomla! is unique, so who knows what would go wrong from user to user. However, it would be nice to offer any input or ideas that might help someone else troubleshoot problems that they are having with the template.

Last, in the `authorURL` tags, place the website address with a page, you feel best encompasses what you want to portray to your target template audience. This is essentially an opportunity to get your URL out there and toot your horn so go on, take advantage of it.

```
<version>2.2</version>
```

You may find that your template goes through some revisions before it's complete, especially if you happen to be working on a team. Perhaps, this is an older template that you've just upgraded and overhauled to run a little more smoothly. If you can apply versioning to this template, go ahead and do so. This is the first version of this look for the template so we'll take it back to version 1.0:

```
<files>
    <filename>index.php</filename>
    <filename>template_thumbnail.png</filename>
</files>
```

OK, everything and anything that is not a CSS, or an image that is *used in the actual template* goes in here. This essentially means your `index.php` file and the thumbnail preview we made at the beginning of this chapter. You must also place any references to JavaScripts you write or JavaScript libraries used by your template. Path information for your files is relative to the *root* of your template, hence, your `index.php` file is just listed. However, if you use JavaScripts that are located inside a folder called `js` you must indicate that path in the filename `<filename>js/moofx.js</filename>`.

Be careful that each additional file is listed inside its own `<filename>...</filename>` tags. We didn't add any JavaScripts so we're good to move on.

```
<images>
    <filename>images/advertisement.png</filename>
    <filename>images/arrow.png</filename>
    <filename>images/button_bg.png</filename>
    <filename>images/contenthead.png</filename>
    <filename>images/indent1.png</filename>
    <filename>images/indent2.png</filename>
    <filename>images/indent3.png</filename>
    <filename>images/indent4.png</filename>
    <filename>images/header_short.jpg</filename>
    <filename>images/menu_bg.png</filename>
    <filename>images/powered_by.png</filename>
    <filename>images/spacer.png</filename>
    <filename>images/subhead_bg.png</filename>
    <filename>images/title_back.png</filename>
</images>
```

All image files that your template uses will be listed within these tags. Again, each image file must be enclosed with `<filename>... </filename>` tags. As mentioned, path information for the files is relative to the *root* of your template. Chances are that you've tucked all your template images inside an `images` folder. Hence, you see the `image/filename.png` path detailed above. If you didn't use a directory called `images` or you've broken your images into sub-directories within your main `image` directory, it's OK. You must still detail each image with its full path: `<filename>images/top-level/filename.png</filename>`. We redesigned and overwrote the original Rhuk images for our template, so we can pretty much leave the image calls alone. However, we did rename our main header image, so we'll replace `header_short.jpg` with our file name, `my_nature_header.jpg`.

```
<css>
    <filename>css/template_css.css</filename>
</css>
```

Last, you'll add your style sheet (or style sheets if you are using more than one). Again, the filename is surrounded with `<filename>`...`</filename>` tags, and its path must be relative to your template's *root*.

Here's what our final template version looks like:

```xml
<?xml version="1.0" encoding="iso-8859-1"?>
<mosinstall type="template" version="1.0.8">
    <name>my_nature_design</name>
    <creationDate>12/22/06</creationDate>
    <author>Tessa Blakeley Silver</author>
    <copyright>my_nature_design by Tessa Blakeley Silver for Packt
               Publishing, remix inspired by: rhuk_solar_flare_ii,
               is licensed under a Creative Commons
               Attribution-NonCommercial-ShareAlike 2.5 License.
                                                </copyright>
    <authorEmail>info@packtpub.com</authorEmail>
    <authorUrl>http://www.packtpub.com</authorUrl>
    <version>1.0</version>
    <description>A simple and stylish template. Based on Rhuk's
                 Solarflare II design for the
                 Joomla! Template! Design! book</description>
    <files>
        <filename>index.php</filename>
        <filename>template_thumbnail.png</filename>
    </files>
    <images>
        <filename>images/advertisement.png</filename>
        <filename>images/arrow.png</filename>
        <filename>images/button_bg.png</filename>
        <filename>images/contenthead.png</filename>
        <filename>images/indent1.png</filename>
        <filename>images/indent2.png</filename>
        <filename>images/indent3.png</filename>
        <filename>images/indent4.png</filename>
        <filename>images/my_nature_header.jpg</filename>
        <filename>images/menu_bg.png</filename>
        <filename>images/powered_by.png</filename>
        <filename>images/spacer.png</filename>
        <filename>images/subhead_bg.png</filename>
        <filename>images/title_back.png</filename>
    </images>
    <css>
        <filename>css/template_css.css</filename>
    </css>
</mosinstall>
```

Zip it Up!

We're now ready to zip up our template files and test an installation of our template package. Zipping is just the file compression type Joomla! prefers. If you're a Windows PC user, chances are that you're very familiar with ZIP files. If you're a Mac user, you're most likely aware of its equivalent, the `.sit` or StuffIt file.

Even if you're working off a server, rather than locally, it's probably best to download your file directories and zip them up on your local machine. Plus you'll want to test your install and mostly everyone will be uploading your file off their local machine through Joomla!'s Administration Panel.

No way to zip? You'll have to take a little tour of the Internet to find the very best ZIP solution for you. There are many free archiving and compression tools that offer the ZIP format. However, we caution you to be careful; we have found some open-source ZIP tools (like a class we used with PHP) that must use an extremely simple or much older set of rules to create ZIP files that Joomla! doesn't seem to like. However, when we use a relatively new compression tool or the trial versions of good old WinZip and StuffIt, the ZIP files they produce seem to upload and work just fine in our Joomla! Administration Panel.

So let's start with the obvious. If you don't have any ZIP compression tools, head over to `http://www.stuffit.com/`. You'll find StuffIt software is available for Mac or PC and lets you compress and expand several different types of formats including ZIP. The standard edition is likely to be all you'll ever need, and while there's nothing wrong with purchasing good commercial software, you'll have plenty of time to play with the trial version. We like StuffIt because, although we primarily work with PCs, we do play well with Macs and being able to create and expand `.sit` files makes us more compatible with our Mac friends. The trial period for the standard software is 15 days but you might find that it lasts longer than that (especially if you're patient while the "continue trial" button loads). If you're on a PC, you also have WinZip as an option: `http://www.winzip.com/`, where again you're given a trial period that does seem to last longer than the stated 45 days.

WinZip and StuffIt are considered industry-standard software, they've been around for a good while, and they are stable products for under $50 (compared to the $700 you might have shelled out for Photoshop or Dreamweaver), so you can't go too wrong.

> **Come on, where's the free Open-Source stuff?** If you want truly free compression software and are on a PC, there is 7-zip: `http://www.7-zip.org/`. We've only minimally played around with 7-zip, but it does create and expand ZIP files and can even compress in a new format (called 7z) that gives better compression than standard ZIP files. Unfortunately, the 7z format isn't compatible with Joomla!, so make sure you're creating a standard ZIP when you use it.

Each compression utility has its own interface and procedures for creating a standard
.zip file. We'll assume that you have one, or have chosen one from above and have
made yourself familiar with it.

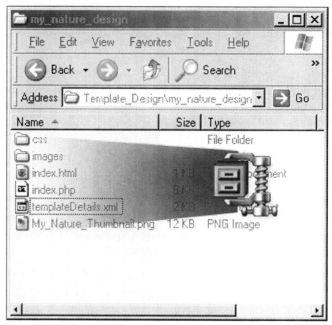

Figure 5.4 Template's root directory to zip

You may want to take one last look at your directory and templateDetails.xml
file to make sure you've placed everything needed for your template structure in the
directory. Once you're sure of this, you can go ahead and compress everything from
the *root* level into a ZIP file.

Uploading to Joomla!

You're now ready to go to the Joomla! Administration Panel, select **Site | Template
Manager | Site Templates** and click on the **New** icon. Then click **Browse** to select
your ZIP file, and finally click **Upload** to begin the installation process into Joomla!.

Hopefully, you will receive a happy **Upload Template - Success** screen:

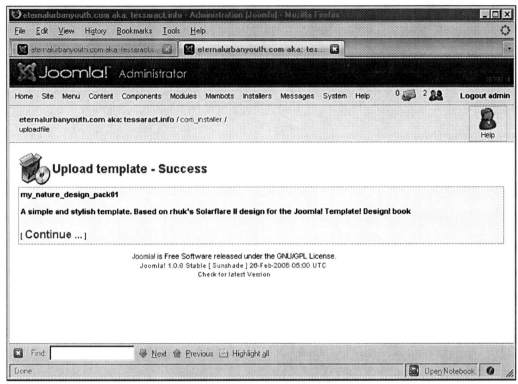

Figure 5.5 Template Upload Success.

If you instead received an **Upload Template – Failed** screen, something was wrong with your package. The good news is that the Joomla! template uploader works a bit like W3C's validator and does a fairly good job of telling you exactly what's wrong with your package.

It will inform you that it **Could not find a Joomla! XML setup file in the package**. If you are sure that you have put your `templateDetails.xml` file in the package, then it's most likely to be invalid because of typos created when adding your files. Check your XML file carefully to ensure that it has all the proper opening and closing tags, all spelled correctly (remember, just like XHTML, your XML closing tags need "/" backslashes).

If that is not the case, Joomla! will tell you what specifically is wrong with
the package.

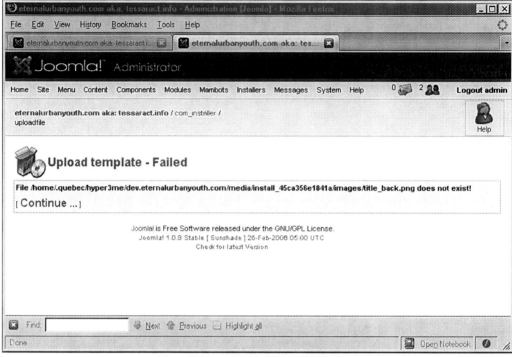

Figure 5.6 Joomla Upload Template Failure

Here in Figure 5.6, you can see that Joomla! has informed us that
.../images/title_back.png does not exist!. When we check our `templateDetails.xml`
file, we do find a reference for this image that is not inside our image directory. It is
an image we're not using, but the reference is a hold-over from basing our work off
the rhuk template. We'll delete the reference from our XML file and add it again to
our ZIP file, overwriting the old `templateDetails.xml` file.

When you uploaded the package again, even though it does *not* show up in the
Template Manager panel, it is likely to have got as far as it could into the process
of uploading and installing. If it managed to create the initial directory, when you
attempt to upload the package again, you'll get a warning saying that directory
already exists.

You must FTP into the templates directory and manually delete the directories and files that were installed by the package. Then, you can go back to the **Template Manager**, select **New**, and attempt the process again. Once you've got a successful file upload message, you can see the template in the Joomla! Template Manager panel. Assign the template to your installation of Joomla! and make sure that it looks good in all the module and component scenarios you've designed it for.

Figure 5.7 Joomla! Template installed and appearing in the Template Manager.

With the successful installation and test of your template, you now have an understanding of the entire Joomla! Template development process from conception to packaging.

Summary

In this chapter, we reviewed all the nooks and crannies of the `templateDetails.xml` file and how to package up your finished template into a working ZIP file that anyone should be able to upload into their own Joomla! installation.

You now know everything there is about getting a Joomla! template design off that coffee shop napkin and into the real world! In the next few chapters, we'll get down into the real-world nitty-gritty of getting things done quickly with our *Template Markup Reference* and *Cook Book* chapters. We'll cover key design tips and cool how-to's. You'll learn how to set up dynamic drop-down menus, best practices for integrating Flash, and more.

6

Templating Markup Reference

Now that you've had some thorough hands-on experience with making templates, you've probably noticed that there's quite a bit of markup that Joomla! spits out. While you can always use your DOM Source Inspector to see what's going on, it's helpful to look at the DOM as well. We'll use this chapter to go over the XHTML markup that Joomla! uses, remind you about how to gain some control over that markup, and look at the standard CSS classes and ID rules that Joomla! references in its markup.

Your Markup and Joomla!'s

You'll remember that in Chapter 3 we started our semantic layout by placing our own markup, which was used as "containers" for Joomla!'s markup. Again, those bits of PHP code that look like: `mosLoadModules('')` or `mosMainBody()` are the ones that end up generating your Joomla! markup.

What You Can and Can't Control

There are many parts of Joomla!'s output that you can control easily, some that you can''t control, and some that you can control with a little bit of creativity. Let's review the list of core Joomla! PHP code, and take a look at the kind of output produced and at the kind of control available.

PHP	Markup Output Produces	Control Options
`<?php echo $mosConfig_sitename; ?>`	plain text, no tags.	You cannot control how this is output. You can just make sure that you wrap the PHP inside span or div tags with the id or class references you customized for display.
`<?php mospathway() ?>`	span tag with the classs `.pathway`	You cannot control how this is output. See the *Classes* table for more information.

`<?php mosMainBody(); ?>`	table tags with some of the following classes:
	`.blog`
	`.blog_more`
	`.blogsection`
	`.modifydate`
	`.createdate`
	`.mosimage`
	`.mosimage_caption`
	`.readon`
	`.contentpaneopen`
	`.contentheading`
	`.buttonheading`
	`.small`
	`.article_seperator`
	`.pagenav`
	`.pagenav_prev`
	`.pagenav_next`
	`.back_button`
	
	Tables house the content title, print, email, and pdf buttons, article content as well as author, date, and next, back, and other navigation.
		You cannot control how this is output. This PHP code can produce a lot of tables and cells depending on the article and or page overview. See the *Classes* table for more information.

`<?php include_once ($mosConfig_absolute_path .'/includes/footer.php');?>`	div tag with a PHP generated year, your mosConfig_sitename, and the PHP generated version of Joomla! you're using.	You can control this, by editing the include/footer.php file. Make sure you're comfortable enough with PHP to understand what you're adding or removing.

PHP	Markup Output Produces	Control Options

`<?php mosLoadModules ('');  ?>`	Tables or `div` tags depending on selected preference, with some of the following ids (depending on the type of module):
	`#mainlevel`
	`#active_menu`
	`#mod_login_username`
	`#mod_login_password`
	`#mod_login_remember`
	`#voteid1`,
	`#voteid2`.. (etc. as many poll items)
	Also, classes (depending on the type of module):
	`.mainlevel`
	`.latestnews`
	`.mostread`
	`.module`
	`.moduletable`
	`.contentpaneopen`
	`.inputbox`
	`.button`
	`.syndicate`
	`.poll`
	`.pollstableborder`
	`.sectiontableentry1`
	`.sectiontableentry2`
		You can control the module output by taking advantage of the `$style` option in your `mosLoadModule` call.
		
		See the `MosLoadModule` `$style` control options table and the *Ids* and *Classes* tables for more information.
		
		Note: The Poll module and Login module will output using the selected `$style` option, but the core content will still be wrapped in tables.

Pretty much the only things over which you have some output control are your module loaders and your menu items. Right off the bat, you'll want to think ahead about what kind of output will be most optimal. Next, let's take a look at our options

mosLoadModule $style Control Options

We discussed these options in detail in Chapter 3. The `$style` option is a numeric value which is placed, after the module position name is called into the PHP code:

```
<?php mosLoadModules ( 'modName', $style);  ?>
```

$style Variables	Effect	Sample

0	Modules are displayed in a table with a single row column. This is also the default setting, so you'll never really need to use it.	`<table class="moduletable"`
		`cellpadding="0"`
		`cellspacing="0">`
		`<tbody><tr>`
		`<th>Title</th>`
		`</tr>`
		`<tr>`
		`<td>Content</td>`
		`</tr></tbody>`
		`</table>`

1	Modules are again displayed in a table with multiple column rows, giving it the effect of being displayed horizontally, rather than vertically like the default.	`<table>`
		`<tbody><tr>`
		`<td align="top">`
		`<table cellpadding="0"`
		`cellspacing="0"`
		`class="moduletable">`
		`<tbody><tr>`
		`<th valign="top">Title</th>`
		`</tr>`
		`<tr>`
		`<td>Content</td>`
		`</tr></tbody>`
		`</table>`
		`</td>`
		`<!--next table cell starts-->`
		`<td align="top">`
		`<table cellpadding="0"`
		`cellspacing="0"`
		`class="moduletable">`
		`<tbody><tr>`
		`<th valign="top">Title</th>`
		`</tr>`
		`<tr>`
		`<td>Content</td>`
		`</tr></tbody>`
		`</table>`
		`</td>`
		`</tr></tbody>`
		`</table>`

$style Variables	Effect	Sample
-1	Modules are displayed in plain text *without* titles.	Content

-2	Modules are displayed wrapped in a single `div` tag, with titles in `h3` header tags. (This is preferred for most applications of Joomla!.)	`<div class="moduletable">`
		`<h3>Title</h3>`
		`Content`
		`</div>`

-3	Modules are displayed wrapped in several `div` tags with titles in `h3` header tags allowing for more complex CSS styling, such as the container techniques that we discussed in detail in Chapter 4, or applying stretchable, rounded corners.	`<div class="module">`
		`<div>`
		`<div>`
		`<h3>Title</h3>`
		`Content`
		`</div>`
		`</div>`
		`</div>`
		`</div>`

Menu Options

In Chapter 3, we discussed changing our menu output to bulleted lists. You have three ways to control the details of your menu output. You can select **Vertical**, **Horizontal**, or **Flat List**. **Vertical** and **Horizontal** will use a table with `tr` and `td` cells to create vertical and horizontal lists. The **Flat List** will create an unordered (`ul`) bulleted list. As the goal of most of today's CSS is to reduce the use of tables and (as discussed in Chapter 4) there are infinite ways to control the display of an unordered list with CSS, the **Flat List** option is probably better.

Go to **Modules | Site Modules** and select **mainmenu**. You'll then notice that you can select the menu's style in the Joomla! Administration Panel. You can do this for all menus created with the **Module Manager**. Select **Flat List**, **Horizontal**, or **Vertical** from the **Menu Style** option.

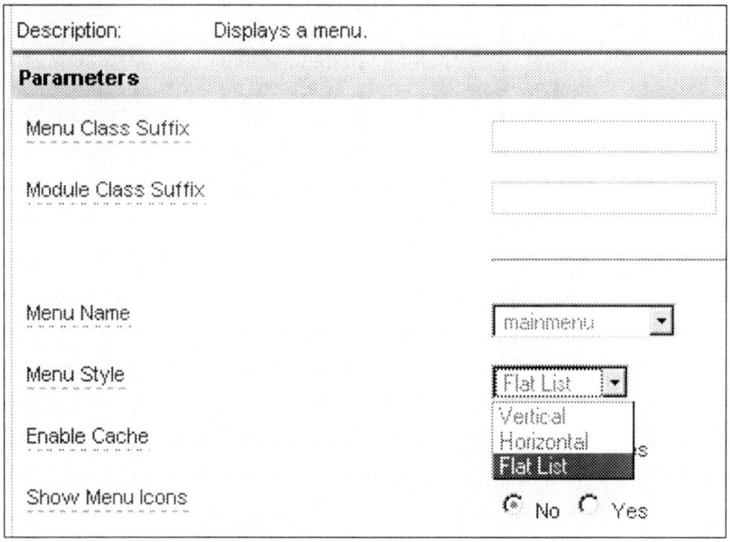

Figure 6.1 Selecting the menu output.

Your CSS File

While some of Joomla!'s output does include standard objects such as h1, h2, h3, a, p, ul, ol, it is pretty much up to you to decide how to style these in your CSS. Below is a list of ids and classes generated by Joomla! (v1.0.x) for which you'll want to be sure to create rules in your CSS. This list has been put together after a bit of research and a lot of Joomla! experimentation. It is probably not complete, but if you account for these items in your CSS rules, you'll be pretty well covered for most Joomla! projects and it will be easy to spot any ids or classes not covered here and add them to your CSS sheet.

IDs

The following table gives a list of different ids along with their description:

Id	Description
#active_menu	This is generated by the mosLoadModules(); code. Use it to style and control the currently selected **mainmenu** item.
#blockrandom	This is generated by the mosMainBody(); code when you're using the wrapper. It is the iFrame's id.
#contact_email_copy	This is generated by the mosMainBody(); code when you're in the contact form page view. This is a field name id.

Id	Description
#contact_text	This is generated by the mosMainBody(); code when you're in the contact form page view. It is a field name id.
#emailForm	This is generated by the mosMainBody(); code when you're in the contact form page view. It is a field name id.
#mainlevel	This is generated by the mosLoadModules(); code. Use it to style and control the main menu div holding each main menu item.
#mod_login_password	This is generated by the mosLoadModules(); code. It is a field name id.
#mod_login_remember	This is generated by the mosLoadModules(); code. It is a field name id.
#mod_login_username	This is generated by the mosLoadModules(); code. It is a field name id.
#poll	This is generated by the mosLoadModules(); code in the Poll module. You can control the placement of the entire id with it.
#search_ordering	This is generated by the mosMainBody(); code when you're in the search form page view. It is a field name id.
#search_searchword	This is generated by the mosMainBody(); code when you're in the search form page view. It is a field name id.
#searchphraseall	This is generated by the mosMainBody(); code when you're in the search form page view. It is a field name id.
#searchphraseany	This is generated by the mosMainBody(); code when you're in the search form page view. It is a field name id.
#searchphraseexact	This is generated by the mosMainBody(); code when you're in the search form page view. It is a field name id.
#voteid1, #voteid2, #voteid3, ...	This is generated by the mosLoadModules(); code. These are generated by the Poll module and are field name ids for the radio buttons.

Classes

The following table gives a list of classes along with their description:

Class	Description
.article_seperator	This is generated by the mosMainBody(); code. Its used to style the space/separations between articles in the blog or news flash views.
.back_button	This is generated by the mosMainBody(); code. It's used to style the main back button which is similar to hitting the back button in your browser.
.blog	This is generated by the mosMainBody(); code if you're in blog view.
.blog_more	This is generated by the mosMainBody(); code if you're in blog view. It indicates there are more blog stories in the links below.
.blogsection	This is generated by the mosMainBody(); code if you're in blog view. It formats additional blog links.
.button	This is generated by the mosLoadModules(); code. Use it to consistently style and control buttons generated by any of the modules.
.buttonheading	This is generated by the mosMainBody(); code if you're in blog view. Use it to control the layout and style of the PDF, email, and print controls.
.category	This is generated by the mosMainBody(); code if you're in blog view. Use it to control the layout and style of links to categories like "Latest News", or "Popular", and "Most Read".
.componentheading	This is generated by the mosMainBody(); code if you're in latest news or blog view.
.contact_email	This is generated by the mosMainBody(); code when you're in the contact form page view. Use it to control the overall placement and style of all the contact form elements.
.content_rating	This is generated by the mosMainBody(); and mosLoadModule(); Code. Use it to style the ratings output of content that has been voted on.
.content_vote	This is generated by the mosMainBody(); and mosLoadModule(); Use it to style the link or button, which allows the user to vote on the content.
.contentdescription	This is generated by the mosMainBody(); and mosLoadModule(); Use it to style the descriptions of content that can be voted on.
.contentheading	This is generated by the mosMainBody(); code. Use it to style the titles of articles and headings.

Class	Description
.contentpaneopen	This is generated by the mosMainBody(); and mosLoadModule(); options. It indicates the start of content.
.contenttoc	This is generated by the mosMainBody(); code. Use it to style the toc listings some content may generate.
.createdate	This is generated by the mosMainBody(); and mosLoadModule(); options. It controls the style of the displayed creation date of the article or blog entry.
.fase4rdf	This is generated by the mosMainBody(); code. It's part of a great type of dynamic formatting class offered and lets you style the news RSS feeds that you can set up through Joomla!.
.frontpageheader	This is generated by the mosMainBody(); code. If you're using the home page module, style the front page headers with this class.
.inputbox	This is generated by the mosMainBody(); as well as the mosLoadModule(); options. Use this to consistently style and control all form fields generated by mosMainBody or a module.
.latestnews	This is generated by the mosLoadModules(); code. The class is wrapped around a list of latest news links, which you can control with additional rule calls: .latestnews td, or .latestnews li depending on the output options you've chosen.
.mainlevel	This is generated by the mosLoadModules(); code. It lets you style and control main menu items displayed in the #maillevel id.
.modifydate	This is generated by the mosMainBody(); code. It accompanies date information if an article has been modified.
.module	This class is generated by the mosLoadModules(); PHP command when using the -3 $style option.
.moduletable	This class is generated by the mosLoadModules(); PHP command when using the 0, 1, -1 or -2 $style options.
.mosimage	This is generated by the mosMainBody(); code. Use it to control and style images placed with articles.
.mosimage_caption	This is generated by the mosMainBody(); code. Use it to control and style image captions placed with articles.
.mostread	This is generated by the mosLoadModules(); code. It is similar to .latestnews. The class is wrapped around a list of latest news links, which you can control with additional rule calls: .latestnews td, or .latestnews li depending on the output options you've chosen.

Class	Description
.newsfeed	This is generated by the mosMainBody(); code in the News Feeds view. Use it to control and style the overall news feed display.
.newsfeeddate	This is generated by the mosMainBody(); code in the News Feeds view. Use it to control and style the news feed displayed dates.
.newsfeedheading	This is generated by the mosMainBody(); code in the News Feeds view. Use it to control and style the news feed headers.
.pagenav	This is generated by the mosMainBody(); code. Use it to control and style the overall placement of next and previous page navigation.
.pagenav_next	This is generated by the mosMainBody(); code. Use it to control and style the next page button.
.pagenav_prev	This is generated by the mosMainBody(); code. Use it to control and style the previous page button.
.pagenavbar	This is generated by the mosMainBody(); code. Use it to control and style the overall placement of next and previous page navigation.
.pagenavcounter	This is generated by the mosMainBody(); code. Use it to control and style the overall placement of the page counter under the navigation.
.pathway	This class is generated by the mospathway(); PHP command.
.polls	This is generated by the mosLoadModule(); PHP option in the Poll module, and you can use it to set alternating backgrounds for your poll select items.
.pollsborder	This is generated by the mosLoadModule(); PHP option in the Poll module, and you can use it to style the outside border of the module. Not to be confused with the .pollstableborder class.
.pollstableborder	This is generated by the mosLoadModule(); PHP option in the Poll module, and you can use it to style the border of the table generated by the module.
.readon	This is generated by the mosMainBody(); as well as the mosLoadModule(); code. Use this to consistently style and control all the "Read More" links for truncated News, News Flashes, and blog items.
.search	This is generated by the mosLoadModule(); PHP option in the Search module, and you can use it to control and style the main search field.

Class	Description
.sectionentry1	This is generated by the mosLoadModule(); PHP option in the Poll module, and you can use it to set alternating backgrounds for your poll select items.
.sectionentry2	This is generated by the mosLoadModules(); PHP option in the Poll module, and you can use it to set alternating backgrounds for your poll select items.
.sectionheader	This is generated by the mosMainBody(); and mosLoadModules(); PHP options. You can use it to control section header titles displayed by modules and content.
.small	This is generated by the mosMainBody(); and mosLoadModules(); PHP options. It's used to denote author names and other data related to an article or blog post.
.smalldark	This is generated by the mosMainBody(); and mosLoadModules(); PHP options.
.sublevel	This is generated by the mosMainBody(); and mosLoadModules(); PHP options. It is used to also denote sub items of navigation.
.syndicate	This is generated by the mosLoadModules(); PHP option. Use it to style the syndicate button layout or boarders of your syndicate module.
.syndicate_text	This is generated by the mosLoadModules(); PHP option. Use it to style the syndicate layout if you're using text instead of buttons.
.text_area	This is generated by the mosMainBody(); option. Use it to control and style the text areas of forms much such as the .inputbox class.
.wrapper	This is generated by the mosMainBody(); option. If you've invoked the wrapper, use it to control and style the iFrame container that the wrapper generates.

Summary

We've now looked at the standard XHTML Markup and CSS classes for Joomla! are and reviewed the standard ways to control what markup is produced via PHP and the Joomla! Administration Panel. Dog-ear this chapter and let's get ready to start cooking. First up: Dynamic menus and interactive elements.

7
Dynamic Menus and Interactive Elements

Some of the techniques that we're about to discuss in this chapter and the next can be used inappropriately and needlessly, and can create issues with usability and accessibility standards, but we're not going to ignore them, because if you haven't already been asked for one or more of these website enhancements, you will be. In this chapter, we'll go over adding drop-down menus to your Joomla! template and discuss various ways of displaying Flash content. It is likely that two out of every five clients have already asked you for drop-down menus, slick Flash headers, and other interactive content tidbits that they insist will give their site some Pizazzz

I find anyone uttering the "P" word extremely annoying. Anyone using this word (or other words like it) is definitely not part of the development or design team. Unfortunately, the people who do use such words, as Steve Krug notes in his excellent book *Don't Make Me Think*, are usually the CEO, a VP, or someone else with money for the project, and where possible, you give them exactly what they want. So Pizazzz it is.

Don't Make Me Think. *A Common Sense Approach to Website Usability* is an excellent book on website design for usability and testing, and anyone who has anything to do with website development or design can greatly benefit from it. You'll learn why people really leave websites, how to make your site more usable and accessible, and even how to survive those executive design whims (without the use of a hammer). You can find out more from Steve's site, which is at http://www.sensible.com/.

Dynamic Menus

This is the nice thing about Joomla!: it's all dynamic. Once you've installed Joomla! and designed a great template for it, anyone with the right level of administrative capability can log into the administration panel and add, edit, and delete content and menu items. But generally, when people ask for *dynamic menus*, what they really want are those appearing and disappearing drop-down menus, they like because it quickly gives a site a very "busy" feel: "Wow, these guys have so much going on, they need drop-down menus to conserve real estate!"

I must add my own disclaimer, I don't like drop downs. It's not that they're wrong or bad; they just don't meet my own aesthetics, and I personally don't think that they are user friendly. I'd prefer to see a menu system that, if it requires subsections, displays them somewhere consistently on the page, either by having a vertical navigation bar expanded to display the subsections underneath, or if a horizontal menu is used, show additional subsections in a set location on the page.

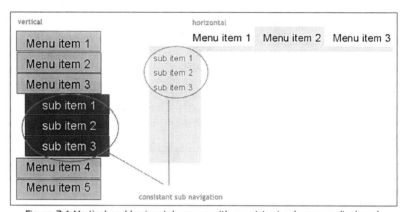

Figure 7.1 Vertical and horizontal menus with consistent sub menus displayed.

I like to be able to look around and say: "OK, I'm in the **New Items | Cool Dink** section and I can also check out **Red Dinks** and **Retro Dinks** within this section". I personally find having to constantly go back up to the menu and drop-down options to remind myself of what's available annoying. If I still haven't convinced you not to use drop downs, read on.

Drop Downs

So you're going to use drop downs. Again, it's not wrong, but I would caution you to help your client take a look at their site's target users before implementing them. If there's a good chance that most users are going to be using the latest browsers, which support current JavaScript, CSS, and Flash standards and everyone has great mobility and is mouse-ready, then there's really no issue, go for it.

However, if it becomes apparent that some of the site's target users will be using older browsers or physical handicaps that will limit them to tabbing through content, you must consider not using drop downs or provide an alternative means of getting through the content such as alternate templates.

 Alternate Templates. You know how to make great Joomla! templates, so why not make more than one? Using Joomla!'s Template Switcher module would enable users to chose a template that displays navigation in a way that lets them tab through the content.

I was especially negative about drop-down menus, because until recently they required bulky JavaScripting or Flash, which makes having a clean, semantic, SEO-friendly XHTML difficult.

The Suckerfish method developed by Patrick Griffiths and Dan Webb of `AListApart.com` is wonderful because it takes valid, semantically accurate unordered lists and using (almost) pure CSS, creates drop downs (IE per usual, poses a problem or two for us, so some minimal DOM JavaScripting is needed to compensate and achieve the correct effect even in that browser.). The drop downs are not tab accessible, but they will simply be displayed as a single, clear unordered list in older browsers that don't support the required CSS, and they will allow for very easy template switching if you allow users alternative options. If you haven't heard of or worked with the Suckerfish method, I would recommend that you read Dan and Patrick's article, which is at `http://alistapart.com/articles/dropdowns`.

I suggest that you play around with the sample code provided in this article so that you understand exactly how it works. Next, we'll look at how to apply this method to your Joomla! template.

SuckeroomlaFish

The essential part of this effect is getting your menu items to show up as unordered lists with unordered sublists. Once you do that, the rest of the magic can be easily handled by finessing the CSS that Patrick and Dan suggest into your template's CSS and placing the DOM script in your template's `index.php` header tag.

As you may recall, in the second half of Chapter 3, we set our **topmenu** and **mainmenu** options to be output as **Flat Lists**, a.k.a. unordered lists. We then styled the **topmenu** to display as a **Horizontal** list similar to what Patrick and Dan described in the first part of the **Style It** section of their Suckerfish article. For this example, I'm going to use my **mainmenu**, which is not a horizontal menu, but you'll quickly see that's OK too.

All we need now are those second level sublists. This is easily done by going to the **Menu | mainmenu** manager in Joomla! and creating additional menu items by selecting the **New** button from the top-right. The key is to just make sure that your *new menu* items have the parent item listed as the *existing* menu item you want them to be under, and not *Top*. You should now see your subitems back in the **Menu Manager**.

Figure 7.2 Submenus

What If Nothing Drops?

In theory, all one would have to do is, go over to **Modules | Site Modules**, select your **mainmenu** or **topmenu** module (or any menu you'd like to apply this drop-down effect to), and make sure that **Menu Style** is set to **Flat List** and that **Expand Menu** is set to **Yes**. This would tell the menu to display in unordered lists and to show all the submenus constantly rather than just when the main menu item has been clicked.

There's just one small problem. *This doesn't work.* It's not just the **Expand Menu** option either: submenus in general simply do not work if you're displaying your menus as **Flat Lists** at this time in Joomla! 1.0.x. (I tried it from versions 1.0.8 to 1.0.12, and got zip, nada, squat.)

Never fear; as is the case with most open-source things, some very clever geek has figured out a solution to this problem and has it readily available for download as a module for Joomla!. Daniel Ecer has saved the day, so head over to his site, and

download the *Extended Menu module* from the download section on this page:
`http://de.siteof.de/extended-menu.html`.

Installing the Extended Menu Module

If you've never installed a Joomla! Module, here's your chance. The Menu module is all zipped up and ready to go. Once you've downloaded it, simply log on to your Administration Panel and head over to **Installers | Modules**. You' should then browse, select the ZIP file, and hit **Upload File and Install**. (It's exactly like installing a template which we discussed in Chapter 5.)

Once you have received the **File Upload - Success** message, you just need to move your menu items over into this new module. No worries, it's easy. If you go to **Modules | Site Modules** and you should see the new **Extended Menu**. Be sure to **publish** the new **Extended Menu** and **unpublish** your previous menu. Now, click on the **Extended Menu** and set your preferences.

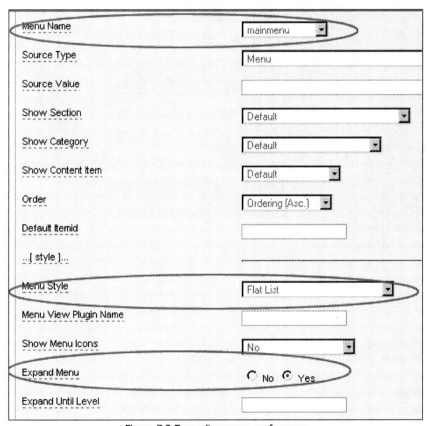

Figure 7.3 Expanding menu preferences

You'll notice that there are over three times as many preferences to choose from as before, but you'll want to make sure that the Extend Menu module is located in the same position as your old menu (in my case, the "main" module location) and that it's assigned to the same menu name that your old menu (in my case, **mainmenu**). Now, you'll want to set your **Menu Style** to **Flat List**. Last, we'll set **Expand Menu** to **Yes** and we should be good to go. Let's check it out:

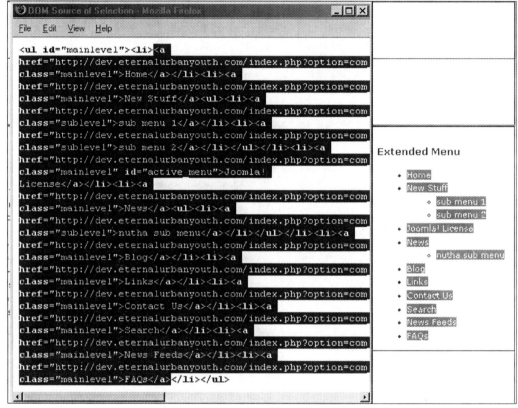

Figure 7.4 Unordered lists with sublists

Selecting the menu and checking the DOM inspector shows us that the menu is in fact being displayed using an unordered list with unordered sub-lists.

Applying the CSS to Joomla!

We're now ready to proceed with the rest of Patrick and Dan's suggestions. To start, let's just take their suggested code and see what happens. The unordered-list CSS that Patrick and Dan provide in their web article is intended to format the sublists as drop-down menus and looks like this:

```
ul { /* all lists */
        padding: 0;
        margin: 0;
        list-style: none;
}

li { /* all list items */
        float: left;
        position: relative;
        width: 10em;
}

li ul { /* second-level lists */
        display: none;
        position: absolute;
        top: 1em;
        left: 0;
}

li>ul { /* to override top and left in browsers other than IE, which
will position to the top right of the containing li, rather than
bottom left */
        top: auto;
        left: auto;
}

li:hover ul, li.over ul { /* lists nested under hovered list items */
        display: block;
}
```

Now, in Joomla!, our menu item's `ul` has an id called **mainlevel**, so Dan and Patrick's code will need to be tweaked in order to work with Joomla!. And there may or may not be lots of other unordered lists used in our site, so we want to be sure that we only affect `ul`'s and `li`'s within that **mainlevel** id. Also, we want our menu list to remain vertical and have our drop downs coming out to the side, so we'll simply tweak the CSS a bit to move items out to the left and add **#mainlevel** to each element in the Suckerfish CSS. The following code takes Dan and Patrick's CSS, and tweaks it to work with our Joomla! template as follows:

```
#mainlevel { /* the mainlevel ul (no need to add ul here) */
        padding: 0;
        margin: 0;
            list-style: none;
}
```

```
#mainlevel li { /* all list items inside ul */
        width: 160px;
            border-bottom: 1px solid #333;


}

#mainlevel li ul { /* second-level lists */
        display: none;
        position: absolute;
            padding-left: 5px;
            padding-right: 10px;
            text-align: right;
            /*these are for IE placement only*/
        width: 160px;
            margin-top: 0px;
        margin-left: -200px;
            /**/
            list-style: none;
            background-color: #ddd;
}

#mainlevel li ul li { /* second level list items in ul */
        border-bottom: 1px solid #333;
}

#mainlevel li>ul { /* to override top and left in browsers other than
IE, which will position to the top right of the containing li, rather
than bottom left */
        width: 157px;
            margin-top: -15px;
        margin-left: -170px;
}

#mainlevel li:hover ul, #mainlevel li.over ul { /* lists nested under
hovered list items */
        display: block;
}
```

Applying the DOM Script to Joomla!

The last bit is the JavaScript that makes the hover work in IE. I call it is the DOM script (as many people do), but it's basically just a JavaScript that rewrites your markup (how your DOM is being perceived by IE) on the fly. Basically, this drop-down effect relies on the CSS `hover` attribute. However, at this time, CSS in IE only recognizes the `hover` attribute if it is applied to (link) entity rules. This script appends our additional `.over` class to the `li` items in IE only.

You'll need to add this script to your `index.php` page's `header` tag. Dan and Patrick named their `ul`'s id **nav**, and that's what this script is looking for. Our `ul`'s id is named `mainlevel`, so if you simply switching out **navRoot = document. getElementById("nav");** to **navRoot = document.getElementById("mainlevel")**; it will work in IE as well.

The full script in your `index.php` page's `header` tag should look like the following:

```
<script type="text/javascript"><!--//--><![CDATA[//><!--
startList = function() {
    if (document.all&&document.getElementById) {
        navRoot = document.getElementById("mainlevel");
        for (i=0; i<navRoot.childNodes.length; i++) {
            node = navRoot.childNodes[i];
            if (node.nodeName=="LI") {
                node.onmouseover=function() {
                this.className+=" over";
                }
                node.onmouseout=function() {
                this.className=this.className.replace(" over", "");
                }
            }
        }
    }
}
window.onload=startList;

//--><!]]></script>
```

For demonstration purposes, I've kept the CSS pretty barebones and ugly, but when we check this out in our browser we now see the following:

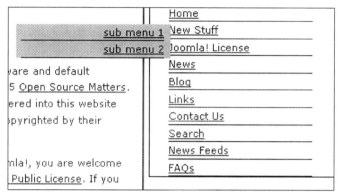

Figure 7.5 Submenu items

It's working! At this point, all that's left is to fix the CSS to make it look exactly the way you want—semantic, SEO, and accessible as possible dynamic menus in Joomla!.

More Suckerfish: Daniel Ecer, the author or the Extended Menu module has made several different Joomla! menu templates that use this SuckerFish method. You can download them from `http://de.siteof.de/extended-menu-templates.html`. Daniel's templates offer unique approaches to using the Suckerfish method, and he also takes advantage of Patrick and Dan's revisited "Son-of-Suckerfish" method, which offers multiple levels and an even further pared down DOM JavaScript. Check it out here: `http://www.htmldog.com/articles/suckerfish/dropdowns/`.

Using Flash

Adobe Flash has come quite a long way since my first experience with it as a Macromedia product (version 2 in 1997). Yet it still does not adhere to W3C standards, requires a plugin to view, and worst of all is a pretty pricey proprietary product. So why is everyone so hot on using it? Love it or hate it, Flash is here to stay. It does have a few advantages which we'll take a quick look at.

The Flash player plugin does boast the highest saturation rate around (way above other media player plugins), and it now readily accommodates audio and video. It's pretty easy to add and upgrade for all major browsers. The price may seem prohibitive at first, but once you're in for the initial purchase, upgrades for the standard and pro software versions are reasonable, and many third-party software companies offer very cheap authoring tools that allow you to create animations and author content using the Flash-player format. (In most cases, no one needs to know you're using the $50 version of Swish and not the $800 Flash 8 Pro to create your content.)

Above all, it can do so much more than just play video and audio (like most plugins). You can create seriously rich and interactive content, even entire applications with it, and no matter what you create with it, it is going to look and work exactly the same on all browsers and platforms. These are just a few of the reasons why so many developers chose to build content for the Flash player.

Oh, and did we mention you can easily make visually slick, super cool stuff that has audio and music in it? Yeah, that's why your client wants it in their site.

The Template

The topmost requested use of Flash is usually in the form of a snazzy header within the template of the site. The idea is that various relevant or random photographs or designs load into the header with some super cool slick animation (and possibly audio) every time a page loads or a section changes.

We're going to assume that, if you're using anything that requires the Flash player, you're pretty comfortable with generating content for it. So we're not going to show you any Flash timeline tricks or ActionScripting. We're simply here to help you get it into your Joomla! template.

For the most part, you can simply take the HTML object embed code that Flash (or other third-party tools) will generate for you and paste it into the header area of your Joomla! `index.php` template file. As long it's positioned correctly, has a correct height and width, and you're not accidentally overwriting any parts of the template that contain `moduleLoader` or other valuable PHP code, you're good to go.

Figure 7.6 shows an object embed tag placed inside the `index.php` Joomla! template.

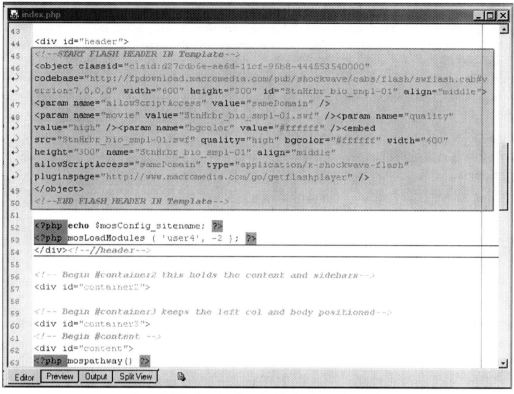

Figure 7.6 Flash embed tags inside `index.php` code

Pass Flash a Joomla! Variable

You've now popped a nice Flash header into your template. Here's a quick trick to make it all the more impressive. If you'd like to keep track of what page your Joomla! user has clicked on and display a relevant image or animation in the header, you can pass your Flash SWF file a variable from Joomla! using PHP. The variable `$Itemid` is used by Joomla! to denote specific page content. If you've set Joomla! to use the standard URL strings you will probably notice something like this:

```
http://mysite.com/index.php?option=com_content&task=view&id=5&Itemid=6
```

If you've set Joomla! to use SEO-friendly URLs you will notice something like the following:

```
http://mysite.com/index.php/com_content/view/5/6
```

In the full URL string you can see the `$Itemid` variable being passed a value of 6. In the SEO-friendly URL, the `$Itemid` is always the last variable (item after a forward slash) shown. So here we can see that the page in question is `$Itemid=6`. Let's say that we have a Flash file that will load a different header randomly but, every time we're on page `$Itemid` 6, we want a special animation to play.

In your Flash authoring program, set up a series of animations or images that will load or play based on a variable set in the root time line called `itemid`. You'll pass this variable to your ActionScript. If the variable *does not* equal 6, then any animation may play, but if the variable is 6, then our specific one will play.

Now, let's get our PHP variable into our SWF file. Add the following to your object embed code where your SWFs are called:

```
<param name="movie"    value="http://fullpathtofile//myswfname.swf
                                ?itemid=<?echo'$Itemid';?>" />
<embed src="http://fullpathtofile/myswfname.swf
                                ?itemid=<?echo"$Itemid";?>"...
```

> Place the *full* path to your SWF file in the `src` and `value` parameters for the embed tags! You can use `<?php echo $mosConfig_live_ site;?>/flash dir/swffilename.swf` too. This just makes sure that your SWF file will load properly.

Now, every time that someone loads a page or clicks a link on your site, this PHP is going to be render out as:

```
myswfname.swf?itemid=6
```

or whatever the `$Itemid` for that page is. So your Flash file's ActionScript is going to look for a variable called `itemid` in the root or level0, and do whatever you told it to do based on that value.

For extra credit, you can play around with the other variables passed to your Joomla! template via Joomla! and load special animations or images based on the section `$task` or `$id` variables passed to your template. Also, you can send *more than one variable* to your SWF by appending them together using `&` (ampersand) characters. For instance:

```
<embed src="http://fullpathname/myswfname.swf
                        ?itemid=<?echo"$Itemid";?>&id=?echo"$id";?>"...
```

There are a lot of possibilities for Flash control there.

Getting Around IE's ActiveX Restrictions

Recently, the IE browser increased its security so that users have to validate content that shows up in the Flash player (or any other player). The animation will kick off, but there will be this grey outline around your Flash content area which may or may not mess up your design.

If your header content doesn't require anything clicked in it, then the grey box is the only problem. If you have content in your header, which can be clicked on or moused over, then the user will have to double-click in the Flash content area first before the content itself becomes clickable. This can confuse some users and make them think your content is broken. You can get around this validation issue by including your Flash content via a JavaScript include. The following two JavaScripts will call the JavaScript code and set the parameters for the code:

```
<script src="<?php echo $mosConfig_live_site;?>/js/flash/loadFlash.js"
    type="text/javascript"></script>
<!--
// Globals
// Major version of Flash required
var requiredMajorVersion = 8;//or whatever version you'd like
// Minor version of Flash required
var requiredMinorVersion = 0;
// Revision of Flash required
var requiredRevision = 0;
// the version of javascript supported
var jsVersion = 1.0;
// -->
</script>
```

You'll also need to add in this VB script which will do some "IE ActiveX magic" (and even I'm not entirely sure exactly what it does, but the `loadFlash.js` file won't work without it):

```
<script language="VBScript" type="text/vbscript">
<!-- // Visual basic helper required to detect Flash Player ActiveX
    control version information
Function VBGetSwfVer(i)
  on error resume next
  Dim swControl, swVersion
  swVersion = 0

  set swControl = CreateObject("ShockwaveFlash.ShockwaveFlash." +
                                                        CStr(i))
```

```
  if (IsObject(swControl)) then
    swVersion = swControl.GetVariable("$version")
  end if
  VBGetSwfVer = swVersion
End Function
// -->
</script>
```

You'll then call the embedded code above within a script like the following, which sets the file parameters and defines your alternative content (content that the user will see if they do not have the Flash Player or have the wrong Flash player version):

```
<script type="text/javascript">
<!--Set your alt content here for people who don't have flash-->
var altContent = '<img src="<?php echo $mosConfig_live_site;?>
                              flash/StaticReplaceImage.jpg" border="0"
                                    width="240" height="311" />';
<!--Calls the actual flash file and passes parameters-->
loadFlash('<?php echo $mosConfig_live_site;?>/flash/mySwfname.swf',
                  240, 310, 'Hope Tree', 'FFFFFF', altContent);
</script>
```

You included JavaScript (loadFlash.js), which will reference the Flash player version that you're testing for and the VB ActiveX script, write the Flash embed tag on the fly to DOM of your pages (very similar to how the SuckerFish menu works in IE), and bypass IE's ActiveX security restriction. The loadFlash.js will look like the following:

```
<!--

function loadFlash(file, width, height, name, bgcolor, altContent){

var hasRightVersion = DetectFlashVer(requiredMajorVersion,
                          requiredMinorVersion, requiredRevision);

if(hasRightVersion) {  // if we've detected an acceptable version

    var oeTags = '<object classid=
                          "clsid:D27CDB6E-AE6D-11cf-96B8-444553540000"'

  + 'width="'+width+'" height="'+height+'"'

  + 'codebase="http://download.macromedia.com/pub/shockwave/
                                    cabs/flash/swflash.cab">'

  + '<param name="menu" value="false" />
```

```
                        <param name="movie" value="'+file+'" />
                        <param name="quality" value="high" />
                        <param name="bgcolor" value="#'+bgcolor+'" />
                        <param name="wmode" value="transparent" />'

        + '<embed src="'+file+'" quality="high" bgcolor="#'+bgcolor+'" '

        + 'width="'+width+'" height="'+height+'" name="'+name+'"
                                                        align="middle"'

        + 'play="true"'

        + 'loop="false"'

        + 'quality="high"'

            + 'wmode="transparent"'

            + 'menu="false"'

        + 'allowScriptAccess="sameDomain"'

        + 'type="application/x-shockwave-flash"'

        + 'pluginspage="http://www.macromedia.com/go/getflashplayer">'

        + '<\/embed>'

        + '<\/object>';

    document.write(oeTags);    // embed the flash movie

    } else {   // flash is too old or we can't detect the plugin

    var alternateContent = altContent;

    document.write(alternateContent);   // insert non-flash content

    }

}//end loadFlash

// -->
```

What's nice about this method is that we account for the occasional user who does not have Flash, in which case they will see a nicely designed static image, which is defined in the "alternate content". This can let the user know they're missing out on the cool Flash content and ask them to get the Flash plugin. However, the actual content experience of the Joomla! site is not halted.

In a Joomla! Page

For content that's going to go into a specific Joomla! page, you're in luck. There's a
Flash content wizard button in the TinyMCE WYSIWYG editor.

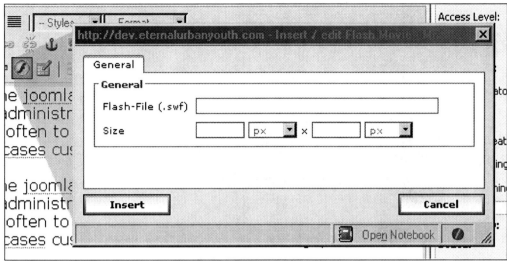

Figure 7.7 Adding the Flash wizard

There's one small problem: again, the button will directly place an object embed tag
into the page with no version check and of course, if the user is browsing with IE,
they will have to click in the **grey box** area. The good news is that the Javascript that
we created above for the header can be leveraged anywhere on your site! You're
already including it in the main template, so the script is available to any content on
your site.

While there is an **HTML** button in your WYSIWYG editor, you may find that once
you save the page, it still overwrites the custom HTML you entered. This is no good.
It will be better to go to the Joomla! Administrator Panel, and change the **WYSIWYG
editor** option on the far right, to **None**. (You may have to get the Joomla! Super
Administrator do this for you, if you do not have Super Administrator access.)

Once you have turned off the WYSIWYG editor, you'll be able to open any Joomla! content page, insert the player version, and `loadFlash.js` scripts above as follows. (The VB script is already in the `index.php` template and you're just referencing the `loadFlash.js` file so the only code you'll need to add is shown in Figure 7.8.)

Figure 7.8 The HTML view

Speaking of Interactive Elements! Add fun and relevant instant updating content to your site! Using the HTML view of the content editor on a page is a great way to add additional fun elements to your Joomla! content. For instance, got a Flicker account? Most community, news, and social application websites offer neat "widgets" that you can place within your own site that are usually served as small JavaScripts. You can copy and paste these scripts into any page or module in the Joomla! site using the HTML view for that content item. Got an AdWords or AdBright account? Paste your Google code directly into your template or into select content pages (for those optimal "hot spots" that they talk about on their site) and start making money on your site!

Summary

In this chapter, we've looked at getting drop-down Suckerfish menus and Flash content quickly and painlessly into your Joomla! site. Next up: getting AJAX with dynamic interactive forms into your Joomla! project.

8

AJAX / Dynamic and Interactive Forms

AJAX is a buzzword that hit the Web in 2005, thanks to Jesse James Garrett, a user-experience expert who founded AdaptivePath.com. (Oddly enough, he's not a JavaScript or XML expert; you can ask him yourself!). If you're totally new to AJAX, I'll just point out that, at its core, AJAX is nothing that scary or horrendous. AJAX isn't even a new technology or language!

AJAX is an acronym for **Asynchronous JavaScript And XML**, and it is a *technique* for using JavaScript and XML to send and receive data between a web browser and a web server. Its biggest advantage is that you can dynamically update a piece of a web page or web form with data from the server (preferably formatted in XML) without forcing the entire page to reload. This technique has made possible for many web developers to make advanced web applications, sometimes called **RIAs (Rich Interface Applications)**, that work and feel more like software applications than web pages.

However, AJAX is starting to have another meaning. For example, a Microsoft web developer may use VBScript instead of JavaScript to serve Access database data that is transformed into an XML stream using a .NET server-side script. Such a site would still be considered "Ajaxy".

In fact, it's getting to the point where just about anything on a website (other than Flash) that slides, moves, fades, or pops up without rendering a new browser window is considered to be "Ajaxy". In truth, a large portion of these sites don't truly qualify as using AJAX; they're just using neat JavaScripts. Generally, if you use cool JavaScripts in your Joomla! template, your site will probably be considered "Ajaxy", despite not being asynchronous and not using any XML.

We're going to look at the most popular methods so that you can get going with AJAX in Joomla! and create interactive and dynamic forms for your Joomla! site. We will also look at some cool JavaScripts and JavaScript toolkits that you can use to appear "Ajaxy".

 Know nothing of this "AJAX" business? The W3Schools site has an excellent introduction to AJAX explaining it in straight-forward simple terms. They even have a couple of great tutorials that are fun and easy to accomplish even if you only have a little HTML, JavaScript, and server-side script (PHP or ASP) experience (no XML experience is required). You can find it at `http://w3schools.com/ajax/`.

Preparing for Dynamic and Interactive Forms

Gone are the days of clicking, submitting, and waiting for the next page to load. A web page using AJAX techniques (if applied properly) will give the user a smoother and leaner experience. If you click on a drop-down option and the checkbox menus underneath are updated immediately with the relevant choices: no submitting, no waiting. Complicated forms that, in the past, took two or three screens to process can be reduced to one convenient screen by implementing the form with AJAX.

As wonderful as this all may sound, I must again offer a quick disclaimer. I understand that, as with drop-down menus and Flash, many of your clients are demanding AJAX for their sites, but AJAX techniques are best used in situations where they truly benefit the user's experience of a page: for example, if they Cut a lengthy web-process form from three pages down to one. In a nutshell, using an AJAX technique simply to say that your site is an AJAX site is probably not a good idea.

You should be aware that, if not implemented properly, some uses of AJAX can compromise the security of your site. You may inadvertently end up disabling key web browser features (like back buttons or the history manager). Then there are all the basic usability and accessibility problems that JavaScript in general can bring to a site.

Some screen readers may not be able to read a new screen area that's been generated by JavaScript. If you cater to users who rely on tabbing through content, navigation may be compromised when new content is updated. There are also interface design problems that AJAX brings to the table (and Flash developers can commiserate). Many times, in trying to limit screen real estate and simplifying a process, developers often end up creating a form or interface that is complex and confusing, especially when the user is expecting the web page to act like a normal web page!

You Still Want AJAX on Your Site?

OK! You are here and reading this chapter because you want AJAX in your Joomla! template. I'll only ask you to take the above into consideration and do one or more of the following to prepare.

Help your client to assess their site's target users first. If everyone is Web 2.0 aware, using new browsers, and fully able to use a mouse, then you'll have no problems, atleast not with AJAX. But if any of your users are inexperienced with RIA sites or have accessibility requirements, you will need to take some extra care. Again, it's not that you can't or shouldn't use AJAX techniques; just be sure to make allowances for these users. You can easily adjust your site's user expectations upfront by explaining how to expect the interface to act. Again, you can also offer alternative solutions and templates for people with disabilities or browsers that can't accommodate AJAX techniques.

Remember to check with *Don't Make Me Think*, the Steve Krug book that we recommended in Chapter 7 for help with any interface usability problems you may run into. Also, if you're really interested in taking on some AJAX programming yourself, I highly recommend *AJAX and PHP* by Cristian Darie, Bogdan Brinzarea, Filip Chereches-Tosa, and Mihai Bucica. In this book you'll learn the ins and outs of AJAX development, including handling security issues. You'll also do some very cool stuff such as making your own Google-style auto-suggest form and a drag-and-drop sortable list (and that's just two of the many fun things to learn from this book).

You're now equally warned and armed with the knowledgeable resources about AJAX that I can think to throw at you. Let's see how to get something "Ajaxy" into your Joomla! site.

Joomla! Extensions

As we've discovered several times in this book, a huge advantage of working with an open-source tool such as Joomla! is that it has a great network of developers associated with it and anyone can contribute. If you've ever thought you needed or wanted something for your Joomla! website, it is likely that someone else has had the same thought and has created a suitable extension that works with Joomla!.

Choosing an extension: Joomla! extensions are a great resource , and the most reliable place to start is at `http://extensions.joomla.org`. There are hundreds of thousands that do incredibly useful things and require no heavy programming experience on your part. When researching extensions, especially those that use techniques that may compromise security, be sure to read all the information about the extension before installing it, including any user reviews provided. As with most extensions offered on the `Joomla.org` site, you should be able to go to the developer's site and probably contact them directly with any questions that you may have about the extension. Be aware that not all extensions are free or Open-Source like Joomla! itself. It will be up to you to decide if an extension is worth paying for.

The type of form that you'll most likely want to use on your site is a comment form. Comment forms are a great way to build a community around your site, not to mention beefing out your content base with user feedback. (This is something to think about if you'll be supplementing the site with Google or AdBrite advertisements. The text that users leave via your comment forms will increase the keywords that will serve up advertisements via these two services creating an opportunity to make more PPC/PPI cash.) Using AJAX techniques within a comment form enables people to post without waiting for the entire page to reload again.

Joomla! Comment 2.40 is an extension that you can add to various pieces of Joomla! content (static pages or regular content pages). It doesn't rate quite as well as some other comment extensions that use AJAX techniques, but at the moment, it's the highest ranking one, and it is free using the GNU GPL license.

You can download it from here:

`http://extensions.joomla.org/component/option,com_mtree/task,viewlink/`

`link_id,677/Itemid,35/`

(Forgive the long URL; you can also just go to `http://extensiona.joomla.org` and search for the extensions by name.)

Installing Joomla! Extensions

Working with Joomla! Comment 2.40 is pretty straightforward. You download the ZIP file and go to **Installers | Components**. From there, you can browse for the ZIP file, and select **Upload File** and **Install** just as for a Module extension.

Is it a module or a component? You'll have to pay attention to the extension's name and instructions to find out if it is a module or a component. (For instance, the Extend Menu extension we worked with in Chapter 7 was a module, not a component). You'll know which installation screen to use. What's the difference? Generally, modules can appear on any page and are usually kept pretty simple. Components, on the other hand, usually load as their own page (or area of a page, the way the Banners component works) and can be more complex.

When you get the **Upload component – Success** screen, you can go to the **Components | Joomla! Comments | Edit Settings** where you'll be able to see the **General**, **Layout**, and **Security** options available for the component.

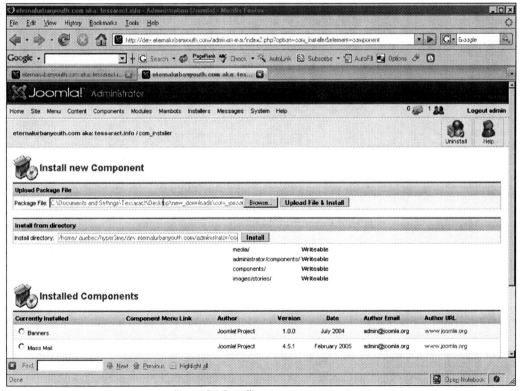

Figure 8.1 Installing a new component

You'll notice that the component will appear on every page unless you specify that certain pages should exclude it.

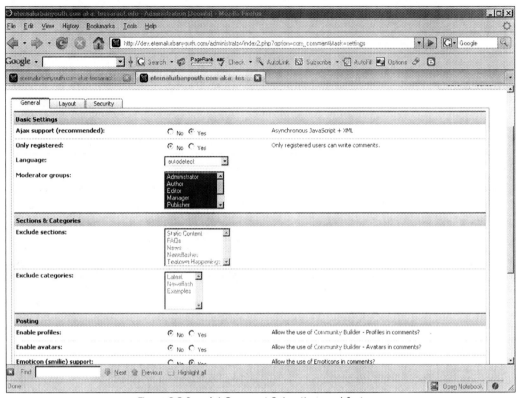

Figure 8.2 Joomla! Comment 2.4 options and features

Using More Than One AJAX Extension Most AJAX Joomla! extensions make use of the XAJAX toolkit. There is a problem running multiple extensions that reference the toolkit—only one Joomla! extension will work. If you're going to install multiple extensions that use this XAJAX toolkit, you'll need to download the solution from http://www.xajax-joomla.com/.

Writing Your Own Extensions If you already have a little AJAX or PHP experience and you feel that it could be reused as an extension in other sites, I recommend that you check out *Building Websites with Joomla!* by Hagen Graf. Chapter 11 will walk you through programming and building your own Joomla! extensions.

Wrapping It Up

What if you're an AJAX/PHP pro and find it easy to build a simple form for a site, but do not thinks that it is worth taking the time to make your own extension? Perhaps the site you're upgrading to Joomla! already had a working AJAX form? Why mess around looking up other people's extensions hoping they come close to duplicating what you need?

Never fear, you don't need to reinvent the wheel by writing your own extension or worry about how you are going to get complicated XHTML markup that references JavaScripts and server-side scripts into a Joomla! content page. Enter the wrapper.

The Wrapper Menu Item creates a content page that wraps an external web page in an iFrame. The iFrame content appears as a "page within a page". Hence, if your content is an external website (such as the `joomla.org` wrapper sample in the "out of the box" installation of Joomla!), then all the site's functions, menus and so on, will be operable from within the wrapper.

There's really no good reason to load someone else's website into your own. However, displaying content that uses non-Joomla! scripts (like your own or existing AJAX scripts), galleries or directories, within your Joomla! template has just got a whole lot easier. You can also use the Wrapper Menu Item to load a page that houses a Flash SWF. (If you don't want to paste the object embed and JavaScript check tags we discussed in Chapter 7, into a content page.) You can also display pages written in specialized web languages that most Joomla! text editors can't accommodate. The wrapper is indeed a wonderful thing.

Remember that we discussed disabling aspects of your browser. The browser's back button only affects the page loaded directly into it and not anything loaded into the iFrame. If a user is working with an AJAX form you've loaded into a page via the Wrapper Menu Item, you'll need to give clear instructions on how to handle the form. For instance, if the user feels they've made a mistake and hits the back button to try to go back and correct it, they'll be taken to the previous content page they (which will be an entirely different page), and not the form's previous state. Make sure that the user understands this, and give them clear instructions about how to navigate through the form's states.

Using the Wrapper Menu Item

Take a look at this tutorial from `W3Schools.com`. It's a great AJAX script that can be used to keep track of a simple CD collection:
`http://w3schools.com/php/php_ajax_xml.asp`.

Watch out! The script above and many scripts that support AJAX nowadays require your server to be running one of the newest versions of PHP (we're using PHP 5.12). If the script doesn't work for you, it gives you an **Unexpected T_OBJECT_OPERATOR** error, and upgrading your version of PHP may be in order.

You may find that a client already has this kind of script in place before choosing to upgrade a site to the Joomla! CMS. Is so, you'll be able to get the AJAX scripts looking and working great with just a minimal amount of work to the front-end XHTML. (Just make sure that you remove the old site's header, nav, and footer includes from the page.) Remember, this is an independent page loading into an iFrame! You'll need to add a style sheet to it, since it will not pick up your Joomla! template's CSS file automatically.

You'll be able to easily integrate many perfectly good existing AJAX applications into their new Joomla! page using the Wrapper Menu Item.

1. Take the script above, which is a basic XML-driven AJAX application that lets us list CDs and Artists (or any existing AJAX form you have access to), and place it on your server.

2. In your Joomla! Administration Panel, go to **Menu | mainmenu** (or any other menu you want the wrapper to be accessible from), and then click **New**.

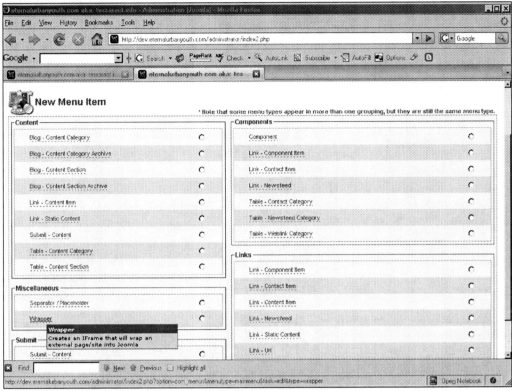

Figure 8.3 Adding a new menu item

3. From the **New Menu Item** screen, select **Wrapper** from under the **Miscellaneous** section.

4. Name the link and include the URL path to the AJAX script.

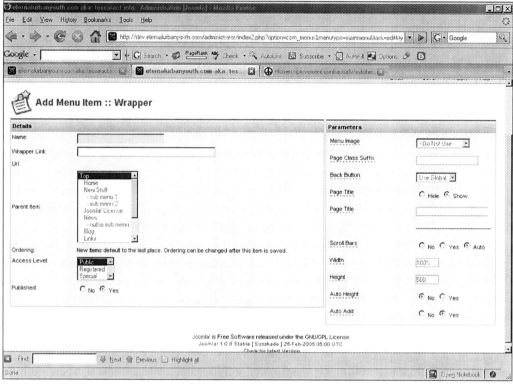

Figure 8.4 New menu item wrapper options

5. In the right panel you can set several different parameters for the wrapper component: height, width, scrollbars, and more.

6. Hit **Save** and your new item should be in the menu you specified.

 Don't want the wrapper content visible from one of your menus? Because this component is a menu item, this is the easiest way to get a wrapper page started. Once you have made the page, click on its link off the menu and copy and save it. You can then unpublish the menu item, but still reference the page from anywhere by referencing the link that you saved.

In Figure 8.5, you can see our XML-driven CD lister loaded into Joomla! via the Wrapper module.

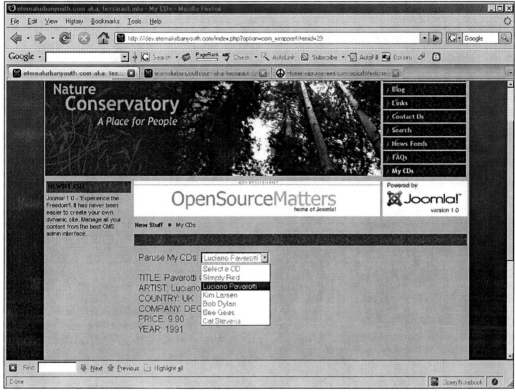

Figure 8.5 AJAX, auto update CD view form

The AJAX Factor

As we mentioned, it's easy to give your site an "Ajaxy" feel regardless of asynchronously updating it with server-side XML, just by sprucing up your interface with some snappy JavaScripts. The easiest way to get many of these effects is to reference a JavaScript toolkit or framework. The two leading favorites in the AJAX community are:

- **Prototype**: `http://www.prototypejs.org/`
- **Script.alico.us**: `http://script.aculo.us/`

Prototype is more of a base framework and `Script.alico.us` is more of a set of libraries for neat effects. In fact, `Script.alico.us` references the Prototype framework, so your best bet is probably to use `Script.alico.us`, but be sure to check out Prototype's site and try to understand what the framework does.

By using toolkits or frameworks such as those above, you will be able to implement their features and effects with simple calls into your Joomla! pages. (Again you will need to turn off the WYSIWYG editor to add custom HTML code that references these toolkits.)

Review the above and choose the one that suits your needs best. Then download and reference it within your Joomla! template's `index.php` header **tags**:

```
<script src="javascripts/prototype.js" type="text/javascript">
                                                    </script>
<script src="javascripts/scriptaculous.js" type="text/javascript">
                                                    </script>
```

JavaScript Components and Libraries

The fun doesn't stop there! There are many other JavaScript-effect components and libraries that are built using the two above. One of the most popular scripts out there that make a big hit on any website is Lightbox JS, which can be found at `http://www.huddletogether.com/projects/lightbox2/`.

This is an extremely easy-to-implement script. After downloading it, add the key scripts to your Joomla! template's `index.php` header file:

```
<script type="text/javascript" src="js/prototype.js"></script>
<script type="text/javascript" src="js/scriptaculous.js?load=effects">
                                                    </script>
<script type="text/javascript" src="js/lightbox.js"></script>
```

Be sure to add the required CSS sheet to the `index.php` file as well!

```
<link rel="stylesheet" href="css/lightbox.css" type="text/css"

                                        media="screen" />
```

Then, you can create a page in the Joomla! CMS, turn off the WYSIWYG editor for your user, and add in basic href links around your image tags as follows:

```
<a href="images/image-1.jpg" rel="lightbox" title="my caption">
                    <img src="images/image-1-thumb.jpg"/></a>
```

That's it! You can also add the page as a wrapper, as we mentioned earlier, but if you leave the greyed-out background turned on in the JavaScript and CSS file, the greyed out area will give away your wrapper's iFrame borders.

Figure 8.6 Shots of JS Lightbox on http://Fransozo.com/home. Site built by http://mediaetc.com

More Joomla! Extensions!

Again, if you have a feature that you think you'd like to use across multiple Joomla! projects, someone else has probably thought of the need too. Don't forget to review the extension's library at Joomla.org to see what's available before cooking up something from scratch.

Here are a couple of good GNU GPL license extensions that can be used to give your site some instant "Ajaxy" slickness (and hopefully "stickyness")

- **SmoothGallery + Lightbox Joomla Mambot**: If you thought that adding your own Lightbox JS galleries to pages wasn't easy enough, then this is a great extension to help out with the easy creation of full gallery slide shows.

  ```
  http://extensions.joomla.org/component/option,com_mtree/
  task,viewlink/link_id,1727/Itemid,35/
  ```

- **Content Items Fading Scroller**: This extension will take multiple published items (under any section or category) and let you display them with a very slick scrolling animation fading on the edges. (It is like a "super-ticker" of the articles and stories you'd like to push traffic to on your site.)

  ```
  http://extensions.joomla.org/component/option,com_mtree/
  task,viewlink/link_id,1003/Itemid,35/
  ```

Both of these items are components, so you'll install them as we installed the Joomla! Comment 2.4 component earlier. Again, both of these extensions aren't true AJAX, but the slick factor is bound to impress your users.

Summary

In this chapter, we reviewed the most common ways to get Ajaxy with your site, and we downloaded and installed two extensions and looked at how to use the wrapper in detail to house an existing, fully-working AJAX application. Up next: some final design tips for working with Joomla!.

Design Tips for Working with Joomla!

9

In this last chapter, let's sum things up by giving you a few final design tips, tricks, and troubleshooting ideas that you can use in your future Joomla! template designs. As we've gone through this book, quite a few tips have been given to you, and here are the top four to remember:

1. **Create and keep lists**: Check lists, color lists, font lists, image-treatment lists from your initial design phase should be kept handy. You'll find them to be useful and an excellent inspiration for your designs to come.

2. **Design for Firefox first and then fix for IE**: Firefox is more than a browser preference; it's a true web designer and developer's tool.

3. **Validate your XHTML and CSS often**: The more stable your markup and CSS, the less hacks and fixes you'll need to make.

4. **Consider usability issues when implementing site enhancements**: Steve Krug is a cool guy.

With that said, let's just go over a few last design techniques that any good designer wants in his or her arsenal these days.

The Cool Factor

In the subsequent sections, I'll go through what I feel are the most popular tricks used in website design today. Most are easily incorporated into Joomla! as they are handled 100% via CSS. A few items will require you to think and plan ahead, as you'll need to make sure the Joomla! template code accommodates the effect. The best thing is that if you can implement these techniques in a Joomla! template, then you can implement them in any website.

Rounded Corners

Rounded corners have been pretty popular in the past few years, to the point that many sites have been accused of incorporating them just so that they seem "Web 2.0-ish". Fads aside, rounded corners are occasionally just going to work well with a design. (They're great for implying happy-friendly-ish tones or retro styles.) So you might as well know how to incorporate them into your Joomla! template.

The Classic: All Four Corners

The classic way to handle rounded corners with CSS is to make sure the module is using the -3 $style selector (discussed in Chapters 3 and 6) and then use the divs Joomla! outputs to set the four corners of the box in place.

Really understanding rounded corners in a table-less design? If you haven't noticed by now, I'm a fan of aListApart.com, so I'll leave it to these trusted experts to give you the complete lowdown on the ins and outs of making rounded-corner boxes with pure CSS: http://www.alistapart.com/articles/customcorners/.

Also, there are many rounded-corner-generator sites out there that will do a lot of the work for you. If you're comfortable with CSS and XHTML markup, you'll be able to take the generated code from one of these sites and massage the CSS into your Joomla! CSS. RoundedCornr. com is my favorite: http://www.roundedcornr.com/.

Use Photoshop or your favorite graphic editor to make four rounded-corner images. This is usually best done by using the square-shaped drawing tool, which also has the option of letting you set the amount of roundedness for your corners. You'll then make slices of each corner and output them as GIF files. You can also generate your images by using the following URL: http://roundedcornr.com. Name your new images: left-bot.gif, right-bot.gif, left-top.gif, right-top.gif and reference them in the following CSS, which will place each image into a corner of each of your Joomla! output module divs:

```
module {
    background: #cccccc;
    background: url(../images/left-top.gif) no-repeat top left;
    /*be sure to set your preferred font requirements*/
}
.module div {
    background: url(../images/right-top.gif) no-repeat top right;
```

```
}
module div div {
    background: url(../images/left-bot.gif) no-repeat bottom left;

}
module div div div {
    background: url(roundedcornr_170953_br.png) no-repeat bottom
                                                    right;
}

module div div div, .module div div, .module div, .module {
    width: 100%;
    height: 30px;
    font-size: 1px;
}
module {
    margin: 0 30px;
}
```

The markup Joomla! outputs with a -3 $style looks something like this. (I've added comments so that you can see which div will have which image associated with it. These comments will not be in your Joomla! output.)

```
<div class="module"> <!--//left-top.gif-->f
<div> <!--//right-top.gif-->
    <div> <!--//left-bot.gif-->
        <div bot right> <!--//right-bot.gif-->
            <h3>Header</h3>
                Content goes in here
        </div>
    </div>
</div>
</div>
```

Using Two Images Instead of Four

This is an advanced technique brought to you by the folks at Compass Designs (http://www.compassdesigns.net/). Its key feature is that only **two** images are used (and yet it scales vertically **and** horizontally). On the whole, it's similar to the four-corner technique, and it still requires the module $style to be set to -3, but if you make your images compressed there's a bandwidth advantage in only having to load two images instead of four.

Create two images: `left-side.gif` and `right-side.gif` following the guidelines in Figure 9.1. Make sure that when the `left-side.gif` and `right-side.gif` are placed together (side by side), the whole rounded-corner image is as large as you would expect any area that uses this effect to be. For example, if the largest rounded-corner area you're expecting to accommodate is 400 pixels wide by 500 pixels tall, make sure that the total of `left-side.gif` and `right-side.gif` equals 400 pixels wide by 500 pixels tall; otherwise, you'll end up with gaps in your rounded-corner effect.

Figure 9.1 Sample left and right side images

You'll then reference these two images in the following CSS, which again, places each image as a background for the module `divs` that Joomla! outputs:

```
module{
    background: url(../images/right-side.gif) top right no-repeat;
    padding:0;
    margin:0 0 10px 0;
    /*be sure to set your preferred font requirements*/

}
module h3 {
```

```
        margin:0;
        padding:0 0 4px 0;
        border-bottom:#ccc 1px solid;
}
module div {
        background: url(../images/left-side.gif) top left no-repeat;
        margin:0;
        padding:6px 0 0 0;
}
module div div{
        background: url(../images/left-side.gif) bottom left no-repeat;
        padding:0 0 0 5px;
}
.module div div div{
        background: url(../images/right-side.gif) bottom right no-repeat;
        padding:0 5px 5px 0;
        height:auto !important;
        height:1%;
}
```

The Two-Image "Cheat"

I'll be honest. I'm on the cheater's bandwagon when it comes to rounded corners. I often create locked-width designs, so I always know exactly how much room my columns can take up. Moreover, I really like using the -2 module $style instead of the -3 $style, as I feel that the less markup the better.

 More A List Apart: Again aListApart.com comes in with a great take on this two-image process along with some great tips for creating the corners in your favorite graphic program: http://www.alistapart.com/articles/mountaintop/.

This rounded-corner fix only requires the -2 $style to be called and **only works** for a **set width** with a variable height. This means that however wide you make your graphic, say 250 pixels wide, that is the **maximum width** that your module can be to accommodate this rounded-corner effect.

So, if you know the width of your columns and just need the height to expand, you can perform this two-image cheat by only making a top image and an extended bottom image as shown below:

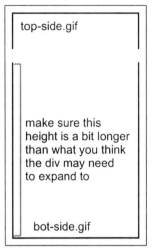

Figure 9.2 sample top and bottom images

Next, reference the images in your CSS so that they are associated with the Joomla! module `divs`:

```
module {
    margin:0 0 10px 0;
    padding:0 0 10px 0;
    width: 150px;
    background:url(../images/bot-side.gif) bottom left no-repeat;
    /*be sure to set your preferred font requirements*/
}
module h3 {
    padding:8px 10px 6px 15px;
    margin-bottom:8px;
    /*be sure to set your preferred font requirements*/
    background:url(../images/top-side.gif) top left no-repeat;
}
```

Great for block quotes! I also use this technique to handle the custom block quotes that are used inside static pages and articles (a great way to spice up pages so that they look "magazine-ish"). Again, the block quotes must be a set width, but I then only need to make sure I place my `<blockquote>` and `<h3>` tags to have an effective style with minimal (and semantic) markup. Just replace the `.module{...` mentioned earlier with `blockquote{...` (or make a special class to assign to your `<blockquote>` tag).

I Don't Want Rounded Corners on all My Modules!

You can customize each type of module by adding its own **suffix**, allowing you to draw attention to a particular module with rounded corners (or any other special CSS).

In the Joomla! Administrator's Panel, go to **Modules | Site Modules** and select the module that you want to focus on in your design (in our case, **Polls**).

Underneath the module's **Details** area, you'll see the **Parameters** area. There, you can create a **Module Class Suffix** to append to that module.

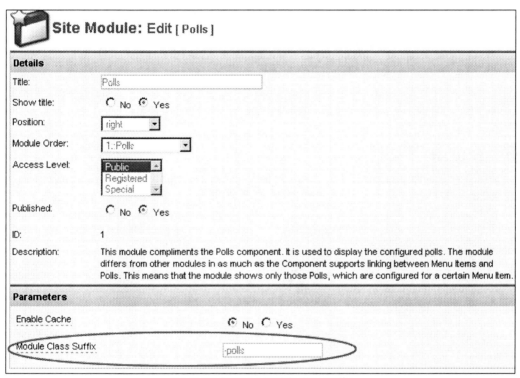

Figure 9.3 Setting a Module Class Suffix

You'll now be able to target that module (and any others that you customized with a suffix) using the specific module-suffix name that you created for it as follows:

```
module-polls {
    margin:0  0  10px 0;
    padding:0  0  10px 0;
    width: 150px;
    background:url(../images/bot-side.gif) bottom left no-repeat;
}
module-polls h3 {
    padding:8px 10px 6px 15px;
    margin-bottom:8px;
    /*be sure to set your preferred font requirements*/
    background:url(../images/top-side.gif) top left no-repeat;
}
```

Now only our Polls module has rounded corners on it, drawing attention to it, while the rest of our site modules have our existing module standards.

Sizeable Text

Sizable text is a fun feature to provide your users with. I'm not big on this feature as being able to size screen text is built in with all browsers. However, many people don't know this and the occasional low vision user will love you as well as the design purist who wishes every website was set in pretty, little 8 pixel type. (Who says you can't make everyone happy?)

First, set a default font size on your CSS body rule. By default, most browsers will set all your text to be *medium* sized. This is roughly like setting your font size to about 16px, which I find quite big.

You'll get around this by setting your initial font size in the body tag to a percentage less than 100% (which again, is about 16px). It turns out that the "atypical" visual designer in me prefers those layouts with tiny type as well (but I try to stop at 10px, not 8px), so I find setting the body tag to about 62.5% works well. (If it's too small, they can resize it; that's the whole point!) Many sample tutorials on the Web like to start you off at 76%, but in reality, you can set it to any percentage you like so long as your basic font size is sensible. (If you like the big type, then go ahead and set it to 100%).

```
body { font-size:62.5%; }
```

Next, you will need to stop referencing your font sizes in pixels (or points or **anything absolute**) from here on out and use the em size unit. By setting your initial size using the relative percentage, you will then be able to accurately size your text up and down from that percentage using the em size unit.

```
div { font-size: .8 em; }
```

What's so great about em sizing? The em size unit refers to the length-size (a.k.a. the horizontal-size) of the font (or other horizontal/length-sized elements you can apply it to). Whether you are offering sizable text or locking your text size in, be sure to pick a size method (em and % or px and points) and then *stay consistent*. You should not be mixing absolute (points or pixels) and relative (em and percentage) sizes together in your CSS. This will cause layout issues down the road. For more information, check out Eric Meyer's article: *Font Sizing*. http://meyerweb.com/eric/articles/webrev/199912.html.

Last, you need to ensure that your layout grows and shrinks with your sized text. You've removed the absolute sizes from your fonts, so be sure not to have any absolute fixed heights on your content div containers. The easiest way to check for this is to view your layout in the browser and using the browser's controls, make the text size bigger and smaller and ensure that your divs grow and shrink with the new text size. You can also do a "Find and Replace" in your CSS for px and pt to make sure that you didn't accidentally leave anything as a fixed font or div height.

Once your template is accommodating all of the above, you will need some graphics indicating that you can make text larger and smaller i.e.: "A+" and "A-", and a "Reset" graphic. You will then need to download the following script. (I'll tell you what to do with it in a second.)

```
http://forum.joomla.org/Themes/joomla/md_stylechanger.js
```

You will need to place that file in the template directory you are using. (As it's a JavaScript file you should have a js directory in your template folder. Also, make sure to **update** your templateDetails.xml file.)

Then, place your A+, A-, and Reset images in your template's image directory.

Keeping the templateDetails.xml file updated If you have not updated it, you should be updating it! Each time you create a new graphic that is going to be used by the `index.php` template and CSS file(s), or add a new JavaScript or CSS file, you must be sure to update your `templateDetails.xml` file. Getting in the habit of keeping this file maintained will make your life much easier when it is time to package the template and hand it over to the client!

Next, paste this bit of code (based on r0tt3n's Joomla! forum FAQ: `http://forum.joomla.org/index.php/topic,36474.0.html`) in your template's `index.php` file in the location *where you want the sizers to be visible*.

This code will display your new text-sizing graphics and when they are clicked, execute the JavaScript code, which resizes the text and makes it smaller and bigger.

Be sure to *update the bold areas* with the correct path and file names:

```
<script type="text/javascript" language="javascript"
                xsrc="<?php echo $mosConfig_live_site;?>/templates/
                <?php echo $mainframe->getTemplate();?>
                /js/md_stylechanger.js">
</script>
<a xhref="index.php" title="Increase size"
                        onclick="changeFontSize(1);return false;">
<img xsrc="<?php echo $mosConfig_live_site;?>/templates/
                <?php echo $mainframe->getTemplate(); ?> /images/
                name of your A+ image here" alt="" border="0" />
</a>
<a xhref="index.php" title="Decrease size"
                        onclick="changeFontSize(-1);return false;">
<img xsrc="<?php echo $mosConfig_live_site;?>/templates/
                <?php echo $mainframe->getTemplate(); ?> /images/
                name of your A- image here" alt="" border="0" />
</a>
<a xhref="index.php" title="Revert styles to default"
                        onclick="revertStyles(); return false;">
<img xsrc="<?php echo $mosConfig_live_site;?>/templates/
                <?php echo $mainframe->getTemplate(); ?> /images/
                name of your Reset image here" alt="" border="0" />
</a>
```

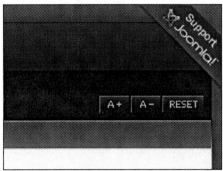

Figure 9.4 Resizable Text Buttons As Seen On Joomla.org

Graphic Header Text

Now here's something that's a total pain for all web designers. There are only three or at the most maybe five truly safe fonts for the Web. You can be fairly sure that every PC and Mac (and maybe Linux) computer has these fonts natively installed. All other fonts tend to be off-limits for web design. This is a shame as typography is a huge element of great design. Nonetheless, if you want these fonts, you have to create them as graphics and include the images in your layout.

The problem with using graphics instead of text—it is usually the headers that you want in the pretty font. However, if you use inline image tags, your semantic markup gets thrown off and your SEO will fall, because SE bots really like to find these header tags to help them assess the real keywords in your page. Also, if your style aesthetic changes, you not only have to change the template but also update individual content pages with new images.

The solution is to use text in your header tags and set up custom classes in your style sheet that will move the text out of the way and insert your graphic font as a background image instead. So your XHTML markup will look like this:

```
<h3 class="newsFlash">Newsflash 3</h3>
```

This is great for disabled people, people who browse using text-only browsers, and let's not forget, our SE bot friends. But, for everyone else, the CSS will place the background image and move the text aside so they see your pretty layout with headers that use your cool font. The bonus is that when the site design changes, all your images are handled via the CSS so you won't have to touch individual article and content pages.

Say you've made a few of these graphic headers:

Newsflash 3

Figure 9.5 Font Graphic

In your CSS, set up the following class rules, which will set up your standard placement and position your graphic-font images:

```
.textMove{ /*this is your standard for each header*/
height: 23px;
margin-top:10px;
width: 145px;
text-indent: -2000px;/*This pushes your text back so it's invisible*/
}

.flash3{ /*specific header-text image*/

   background: url("../images/flash3.jpg") no-repeat left top;

}
```

In your Joomla! Administration Panel, for the content pages you'd like to apply this technique, apply the appropriate class to the header(s) that you place in the body text area of the editor. (Again, turn off the WYSIWYG editor to do this.)

```
<h2 class="noHead flash3">Newsflash 3</h2>
```

 Assign more than one class rule to an XHTML markup object. As you can see from our sample above, you can assign more than one class rule to a markup object. Simply separate each class rule with a **space** (not a comma) e.g.: class="rule1 rule2". This comes in handy when you need to customize many elements, but don't want to repeatedly copy similar properties across all of them. (Also, you can easily change the main properties in just one place instead of having to fix them all.) In the case of graphic-text headers, I like to make one rule that handles pushing the text out of the way and sets the height and margins for my header images so that all my other class rules just handle the background image name: class="textMove moreText".

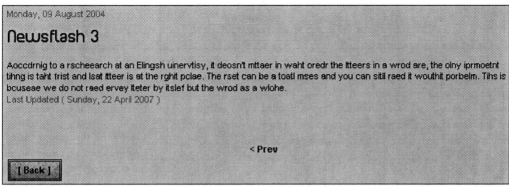

Figure 9.6 Header Graphic In Page

What about my Module headers? You need to be able to control an id or class attribute in a `table` or `div` tag, in order to call in a background graphic via CSS. That's why it's so easy for us to place consistent background images behind our module headers, but targeting them to place actual graphic text takes a little extra effort. To use this trick with module headers you will need to give each module a special suffix (please refer to the *Rounded Corners* section) and then target the h3 tag under that module-suffix: `.module-suffixName h3 {`. . . . Of course, you can't target your module headers with two classes as we did in our above example but you will still get your graphic-font in there.

Note: This technique can get a little complicated if you want rounded corners on the module and a graphic header, but as you're creative, you'll quickly see how to accommodate that (please refer *The Two-Image "Cheat"* section). For headers used in page content, I just turn off the **Show Title** feature available for many module and content items and add the header manually to the content text area.

Using PHP to Make Graphic Headers Easy

I like to simplify this process by using a simple PHP script with a local **TTF (True-Type Font)** font to help me quickly generate my header graphics. I can then just include them into my CSS sheet, dynamically setting up the text that the header needs to say.

This technique is very useful if your site is going to be mainly controlled by a client, as they will probably have to let you know every time they make a new header that needs to be a graphic loaded in via CSS. You will be able to accommodate them on the fly (or even better, teach them how to do it) as opposed to having them wait for you to generate the graphic with Photoshop or Gimp and then implement the CSS.

Heads up: This PHP code requires the standard **ImageGD** library to be installed with your PHP configuration. (Contact your website host administrator to ensure the ImageGD library is installed.)

You can place this script's file anywhere you like. I usually place a script like this in my template's image directory as I will be referencing them as images (again, update your templateDetails.xml file).

imgtxt.php:

```php
<?php

/*Basic JPG creator by Tessa Blakeley Silver.
Free to use and change. No warranty.
Author assumes no liability, use at own risk.*/

header("Content-type: image/jpeg");

$xspan = $_REQUEST['xspan'];//if you want to adjust the width
$wrd = $_REQUEST['wrd'];//what the text is

if (!$xspan){//set a default width
    $xspan = 145;
}

$height = 20;//set a default height

$image = imagecreate($xspan, $height);

//Set your background color.
//set to what ever rgb color you want
if(!$bckCol){
    $bckCol = imagecolorallocate($image, 255, 255, 255);
}
```

```
//make text color, again set to what ever rgb color you want
if (!$txtCol){
    $txtCol = imagecolorallocate($image, 20, 50, 150);
}

//fill background
imagefilledrectangle($image, 0, 0, $xspan, $height, $bckCol);

//set the font size on the 2nd parameter in
//set the server path (not the url path!) to the font location at the
//7th parameter in:
imagettftext($image, 15, 0, 0, 16, $txtCol,
"home/user/sitename/fonts/PLANE___.TTF", "$wrd");//add text


imagejpeg($image,'',80);//the last number sets the jpg compression

//free up the memory allocated for the image.
imagedestroy($image);

?>
```

> This script only works with **TrueType fonts**. This PHP script is written to generate an image with a background color of your choice and the TrueType font you specify, in the color of your choice. Upload the TrueType font and directory location that you referenced in the script to the matching location on the server.

From here on, you will only need to reference this PHP script in your CSS, passing your text to it via a query string instead of the images that you were generating:

```
flash3{
    background: url("../images/imgtxt.php?xspan=300&wrd=Newsflash 3")
                                            no-repeat left top;
}
```

Each time you have a new graphic to generate, you can do it entirely via the template's style sheet and the Joomla! Administration Panel.

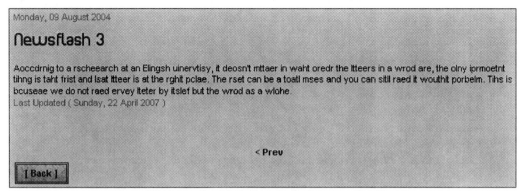

Figure 9.7 Header Graphic In Page. Looks the same. But it's not!

 Additional Template Tricks and Tutorials: Compass Designs (the creator of the first two-image technique) makes professional, commercial Joomla! templates. (You pay for them, but they are really nice templates.) Compass Designs is also great in that they share knowledge liberally with the community. If you'd like to learn more design tricks for Joomla! check out their site's tutorial section:

`http://www.compassdesigns.net/tutorials/`
`joomla-tutorials/.`

Advanced Tips

At this point you can get just about anything you can imagine into your Joomla! template and site. In this last section we will just go over a few final advanced tips and tricks, and some troubleshooting items you are bound to run into (eventually, anyway).

Common WYSIWYG Editor Issue

Imagine this scenario. You have designed the most beautiful, slickest, coolest Joomla! site ever. Congratulations. It's complete with an awesome, rich, dark background. Instead of fawning over your great masterpiece, the client calls you back complaining that they can't add or edit content because the editing area is filled with your rich, dark background. You, who turned off your WYSIWYG editor so you could add in Flash, AJAX techniques, or Lightbox JS code, didn't notice this.

Basically, the Tiny MCE editor that comes with Joomla! and the third-party editor, JCE (Joomla! Content Editor), both pull the `template_css.css` sheet so that content editors can style their text with a pull-down menu of CSS style. The style sheet is also applied to the edit area window. On the whole, this makes the What-You-See-Is-What-You-Get, a little more accurate (which is a good thing). This is fine if you have a white or very, very light background color assigned to your CSS body rule, but if you have a dark background color or repeating image assigned to the body rule, the background of your WYSIWYG edit pane takes on that color, or image repeat (which is a bad thing).

This gets particularly troublesome as you will generally have the text inside a content container `div` that has a lighter background color assigned to it, with a dark font color over that. This content container `div` isn't present in the editing window and the general result is a dark background color with dark text over it in the edit pane:

Figure 9.8 Impossible To Edit!

There's an easy fix for this, the TinyMCE editor, which only sniffs out the `template_css.css` sheet. So anything that isn't in that style sheet will not affect the WYSIWYG edit area. Simply remove your body rule from the `template_css.css` sheet and place it in a separate style sheet: `body.css`. If by some chance you notice other styles are adding confusion to your WYSIWYG edit pane, you can remove those as well and add them to the new style sheet. You then just have to make sure that your `index.php` file calls in *both* the style sheets. (If you are also including IE fix style sheets this is nothing new to you.)

Once you made this fix, be sure that your `templateDetails.xml` file is updated to accommodate the additional style sheet! Also, a developer's comment in the main `template_css.css` sheet would be nice in case the Joomla! site ever has another designer or developer working with it.

What About SEO?

At this point you've gone through the trouble to create a semantic, user-friendly, accessible XHTML template structure and one of the benefits of this structure is that it helps with **SEO** (**Search Engine Optimization**, if you haven't guessed by now). You might as well go all out and take advantage of the built-in SEO features Joomla! has to offer.

URLs

Joomla! URLs are dynamic by default. This means they are a query string of the `index.php` page: `index.php?option=com_poll&task=results&id=14`.

In the past, dynamic URLs had been known to break SE bots that either didn't know what to do when they hit a question mark or ampersand or started indexing entire sites as "duplicate content" because everything looked like it was coming from the same page (the `index.php` page). Generally, this is no longer the case, at least not with the "big boy" search engines but you never know who is searching for you using what service.

Also, by changing the dynamic string URL to a more **SEF** (**Search Engine Friendly**) URL, its a little harder for people to directly manipulate your URLs because they can't clearly see which variable they're changing once it's in an SEF URL.

Joomla! has this SEF URL feature built-in (but **only** if you're running PHP on Apache). First, you have to go into the root of your Joomla! installation and change the name of your `htaccess.txt` file to just `.htaccess`.

Next, in your user administration panel go to **Site | Global Configuration** and click on the **SEO** tab. Under **Search Engine Friendly URLS**, select **Yes**. You'll notice that your URLs now display something more along the lines of: `index.php/com_poll/results/14/`.

SE bots will think the forward slashes are directories and not freak out about question marks and ampersands or assume that everything on your site is really the same page.

Forget the SE bots! What about People Friendly URLs? Yes, that is a problem with the current 1.0.x version. It's not exactly easy to just tell someone where your hot new article is, if it's a series of forward slashes, bizarre abbreviated words, and numbers. Also clearly named URLs greatly boost your link trust (that's what I call it anyway). If the link you've emailed people or posted in your blog doesn't appear to clearly have any indication of what you have promised to be in it, people are much less likely to click on it. Even though the impact of keywords in URLs seems to be waning, there are SEO experts who still swear that your URLs should contain the top keywords in your document. ARTIO JoomSEF is a third-party component that's helpful in cleaning up Joomla! URLS into "PF" URLs.

`http://www.artio.cz/en/joomla-extensions/artio-joomsef`

Keywords and Descriptions

The effectiveness of placing keywords into your meta-tags is now widely disputed. (Since it's so easily subject to misuse and manipulation, there's even speculation that perhaps the big search engines don't reference this meta tag at all anymore.) I therefore feel that it's still wise to place your major keywords into a tag. (Again if nothing else, the smaller, lesser-known search engines may still use them.) I'm not so big on targeting misspellings anymore as the major search engines compensate for misspellings but some people still say it's important. (Don't you just love the "exact science" of SEO?)

However, I do find a well-written meta description useful as it seems search engines may randomly choose to display your meta description instead of the relevant bit of text on the page that pertains to the keyword search someone just performed.

When it comes to these two meta tags, I'm an advocate of "less is more". Do not drop in 200 keywords and a four paragraph description into your meta tags. Simply put in the top 5 to 10 keywords used in your article or page, as well as a one sentence description (or possibly two sentences) that contains at least 3 to 5 of those keywords. Anything more than that, and I believe the GoogleMonster will assume you're trying to pull some SEOBlackHat stunt and ignore fully indexing your pages.

You may have noticed in your Joomla! Administration Panel, when you edit or create a new content page (be it an article, static page or even a wrapper) there's a side panel off to the right.

If you click the **Meta Info** tab, you'll have two areas to include your content page's description and keywords.

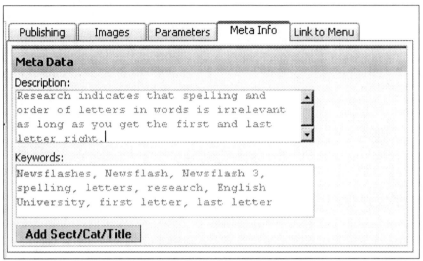

Figure. 9.9 Meta Info Panel in Edit Content Screen

For advanced SEO control over your content and help with generating keywords and meta tags (which is always a pain to do), there's an excellent plug-in extension that I've found useful called JoomlaSEO. You can get it from here: http://www.joomseo.com/.

Ways to Remove More Tables from Joomla!

Throughout the course of this book, we've showed you how to remove as many tables as possible from your Joomla! design. At this point, there are probably no tables in your template at all, however, anything that is output in the mainBody(); tag is still going to be wrapped in several tables.

If you feel at this point, you're quite the Joomla! template pro and you really want to try and go for an all table-less layout or you are unhappy with certain aspects that the mainBody(); tosses out at you, you can modify it.

Warning: If you're going to open this file and muck around in it, do the following:

1. Back up the file so that you can revert back to it if you break it.

2. Make sure that you are comfortable and understand the difference between HTML markup and PHP code.

3. Only touch the HTML markup and not any of the PHP code (unless you're also a PHP wizard and intentionally want to change it, in which case, make sure that you did Step 1 before you change it).

4. Remember, any changes you make to these files will probably be lost if you ever upgrade your Joomla! installation (so have an upgrade plan if the changes are crucial).

In your Joomla! root directory, locate the following directory and file:

`/components/com_content/content.html.php`.

In this file you'll see the entire table code that Joomla! uses to wrap content in. Here you can strip and replace `table` tags for `div` tags as you see fit. For example, the following code comes from the `content.html.php` file (starting on line 41 and continuing to line 64):

```php
if ( $params->get( 'page_title' ) ) {
        ?>
        <div class="componentheading<?php echo $params->
                                    get( 'pageclass_sfx' ); ?>">
        <?php echo $title->name; ?>
        </div>
        <?php
}
?>
<table width="100%" cellpadding="0" cellspacing="0"
                    border="0" align="center"
                    class="contentpane<?php echo $params->
                    get( 'pageclass_sfx' ); ?>">
<tr>
    <td width="60%" valign="top"
            class="contentdescription<?php echo $params->
            get( 'pageclass_sfx' ); ?>" colspan="2">
    <?php
    if ( $title->image ) {
        $link = $mosConfig_live_site .'/images/stories/'
                                    $title->image;
```

```
        ?>
        <img src="<?php echo $link;?>" align="
                        <?php echo $title->image_position;?>
                        " hspace="6" alt="
                        <?php echo $title->image;?>" />
            <?php
        }
        echo $title->description;
        ?>
        </td>
    </tr>
    <tr>
        <td>(... code continues)
```

By leaving the PHP in place, you can see how to remove the table and table cells to insert more friendly XHTML structures.

More Ways to Edit Joomla's XHTML Markup

While we're here poking around the /components/ directory, you will find many other com_componentName folders: from com_banners to com_wrapper. Inside each of these directories, you may or may not find a componentName.html.php file.

The files that have html in their name are output files that contain the HTML markup that Joomla! uses to wrap content in. You can edit these files just like the content.html.php file that we described earlier.

Remember, everything in the /compontents/ folder only affects items output by the mainBody(); code. For example, if you edit the polls.html.php file, the Polls displayed in your side bar will not be affected. Only the Polls Results display (which shows up in your mainBody();) will change. Again, unless you are a bonafide PHP wiz and know exactly what you're doing, be careful with these files, follow the steps in the information box above, and only work with components that offer componentName.html.php files.

Final Note On Customizing the mainBody();

There is one last thing to consider before you indiscriminately start stripping down the markup of your Joomla! mainBody(); output: The Joomla! CMS was put together by a great Joomla! team of expert PHP coders and web developers with some careful thought. Therefore, they probably had many good reasons for including the core component code and markup that they did. Just be aware that changing this output in any way can affect how the Joomla! CMS works and looks on the whole. For instance, if your site's editors and contributors are going to be heavily reliant on the WYSIWYG editor (which is very likely), keep in mind that some of the markup produced by the editor may not look good if it's not contained in a table. Be prepared to do lots of testing if you customize any of these files to make sure that the content display and site features continue working and look as everyone expects them to.

Summary

There you have it—all there is to know about making templates with Joomla!. In this chapter we reviewed the main tips you should have picked up from the previous chapters as well as covered some key tips for easily implementing today's coolest CSS tricks into your template. We also looked at a few final fix them tips that you would probably run into once you turn the site over to the content editors. I hope you've enjoyed this book and found it useful in aiding your Joomla! template creations.

This appendix contains the CSS and XHTML code used to generate the two designs created in Chapter 3. Rhuk Redesign is just the `template_css.css` style sheet as none of the XHTML in the `index.php` file needs to be touched. Table-less CSS contains the `template_css.css` as well as the XHTML and PHP code placed in the main `index.php` file.

Rhuk Redesign

The following CSS code was based on the original `rhuk_solarflare_ii` template to generate the first version of the Rhuk Redesign in Chapter 3:

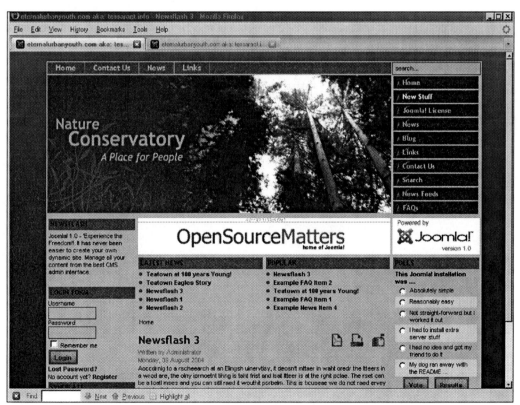

Figure A.1: The redesigned rhuk_solarflare_ii template

The CSS

```
html {
    height: 100%;
}

body {
    height: 100%;
      margin: 15px;
      margin-bottom: 1px;
      padding: 0px;
      font-family: Arial, Helvetica, Sans Serif;
      line-height: 120%;
      font-size: 11px;
      color: #333333;
      background: #070706 url(../images/main_bg.jpg) repeat-x fixed
                                                         top left;
}

clr {
    clear: both;
}

outline {
    border: 1px solid #586230;
    background: #e3dabd;
    padding: 2px;
}

#buttons_outer {
    width: 635px;
  margin-bottom: 2px;
    margin-right: 2px;
    float: left;

}

#buttons_inner {
    height: 21px;
    background: #586230;
    background-image: url(../images/subhead_bg.png);
}

#pathway_text {
```

```
    overflow: hidden;
      display: block;
      height: 25px;
      line-height: 25px !important;
      line-height: 22px;
      padding-left: 4px;
      margin-bottom: 2px;
}

#pathway_text img {
    margin-left: 5px;
    margin-right: 5px;
    margin-top: 6px;
}

#buttons {
    float: left;
    margin: 0px;
    padding: 0px;
    width: auto;
}


ul#mainlevel-nav{
    list-style: none;
    padding: 0;
    margin: 0;
    font-size: 0.8em;
}

ul#mainlevel-nav li{
    padding-left: 0px;
    padding-right: 0px;
    float: left;
    margin: 0;
    font-family: Trebuchet MS, Helvetica, Arial;
    font-size: 14px;
    line-height: 21px;
    white-space: nowrap;
    border-right: 1px solid #e3dabd;
    background-image: none;
}

ul#mainlevel-nav li a{
```

```
        display: block;
        padding-left: 15px;
        padding-right: 15px;
        text-decoration: none;
        color: #e3dabd;
        background: transparent;
}

#buttons>ul#mainlevel-nav li a { width: auto; }

ul#mainlevel-nav li a:hover{
        color: #586230;
        background: #e3dabd;
}


#search_outer {
        float: left;
        width: 165px;
}

#search_inner {
      border: 1px solid #586230;
        padding: 0px;
      height: 21px !important;
      height: 23px;
      overflow: hidden;
}

#search_inner form {
      padding: 0;
      margin: 0;
}

#search_inner .inputbox {
        border: 0px;
        padding: 3px 3px 3px 5px;
        font-family: arial, helvetica, sans-serif;
        font-size: 11px;
        color: #2C2014;
}

#header_outer {
        text-align: left;
```

```
    border: 0px;
    margin: 0px;
}

#header {
    float: left;
    padding: 0px;
    margin-right: 2px;
    width: 635px;
    height: 250px;
    background: url(../images/my_nature_header.jpg) no-repeat;
}

#top_outer{
    float: left;
    width: 165px;
}

#top_inner {
    padding: 2px;
  height: 250px !important;
  height: 256px;
  overflow: hidden;
  float: none !important;
  float: left;
}

#left_outer {
  float: left;
    margin-top: 2px;
    width: 165px;
}

#left_inner {
    padding: 2px;
  float: none !important;
  float: left;
}

#content_outer {
    padding: 0px;
    margin-top: 0px;
    margin-left: 2px;
    /** border: 1px solid #cccccc; **/
```

```
      float: left;
      width: 635px;
}

#content_inner{
   float: none !important;
   float: left;
   padding: 0;
   padding-top: 2px;
   margin: 0;
}

table.content_table {
   width: 100%;
      padding: 0px;
      margin: 0px;
}

table.content_table td {
      padding: 0px;
      margin: 0px;
}


#banner_inner {
      float: left;
      padding: 0px;
      height: 70px;
}


#poweredby_inner {
      float: right;
      padding: 0px;
      margin-left: 0px;
      height: 70px;
}

#right_outer {
      margin-left: 2px;
      width: 165px;
}
```

```
#right_inner {
  float: none !important;
  float: left;
  padding: 2px;
}


.user1_inner {
  float: none !important;
  float: left;
    margin: 0px;
    padding: 2px;
}

.user2_inner {
  float: none !important;
  float: left;
    margin: 0px;
    padding: 2px;
}

table td.body_outer {
    padding: 2px;
}

maintitle {
    color: #ffffff;
    font-size: 40px;
    padding-left: 15px;
    padding-top: 20px;
}

.error {
  font-style: italic;
  text-transform: uppercase;
  padding: 5px;
  color: #cccccc;
  font-size: 14px;
  font-weight: bold;
}

/** old stuff **/

.back_button {
```

```
      float: left;
    text-align: center;
    font-size: 11px;
    font-weight: bold;
    border: 3px double #586230;
    width: auto;
    background: url(../images/button_bg.png) repeat-x;
    padding: 0px 10px;
    line-height: 20px;
    margin: 1px;
}

.pagenav {
    text-align: center;
    font-size: 11px;
    font-weight: bold;
    border: 3px double #586230;
    width: auto;
    background: url(../images/button_bg.png) repeat-x;
    padding: 0px 10px;
    line-height: 20px;
    margin: 1px;
}

.pagenavbar {
    margin-right: 10px;
    float: right;
}

#footer {
    text-align: center;
    padding: 3px;
}

ul{
margin: 0;
padding: 0;
list-style: none;
}

li{
line-height: 15px;
padding-left: 15px;
padding-top: 0px;
```

```
background-image: url(../images/arrow.png);
background-repeat: no-repeat;
background-position: 0px 2px;
}


td {
    text-align: left;
    font-size: 11px;
}


/* Joomla core stuff */
a:link, a:visited {
    color: #586230; text-decoration: none;
    font-weight: bold;
}

a:hover {
    color: #918B73;    text-decoration: none;
    font-weight: bold;
}

table.contentpaneopen {
  width: 100%;
    padding: 0px;
    border-collapse: collapse;
    border-spacing: 0px;
    margin: 0px;
}

table.contentpaneopen td {
    padding-right: 5px;
}

table.contentpaneopen td.componentheading {
    padding-left: 4px;
}


table.contentpane {
  width: 100%;
    padding: 0px;
```

```
        border-collapse: collapse;
        border-spacing: 0px;
        margin: 0px;
}

table.contentpane td {
        margin: 0px;
        padding: 0px;
}

table.contentpane td.componentheading {
        padding-left: 4px;
}

table.contentpaneopen fieldset {
        border: 0px;
        border-bottom: 1px solid #eee;
}

.button {
    color: #586230;
    font-family: Arial, Hevlvetica, sans-serif;
    text-align: center;
    font-size: 11px;
    font-weight: bold;
    border: 3px double #586230;
    width: auto;
    background: url(../images/button_bg.png) repeat-x;
    padding: 0px 5px;
    line-height: 18px !important;
    line-height: 16px;
    height: 26px !important;
    height: 24px;
    margin: 1px;
}

.inputbox {
        padding: 2px;
        border:solid 1px #34300A;
        background-color: #e3dabd;
}

.componentheading {
        background: url(../images/subhead_bg.png) repeat-x;
```

```
        color: #666666;
        text-align: left;
        padding-top: 4px;
        padding-left: 4px;
        height: 21px;
        font-weight: bold;
        font-size: 10px;
        text-transform: uppercase;

}

.contentcolumn {
        padding-right: 5px;
}

.contentheading {
        height: 30px;
        font-family: Trebuchet MS, Helvetica, Arial;
        color: #586230;
        font-weight: bold;
        font-size: 20px;
        white-space: nowrap;
}

.contentpagetitle {
        font-size: 13px;
        font-weight: bold;
        color: #cccccc;
        text-align:left;
}

table.searchinto {
        width: 100%;
}

table.searchintro td {
        font-weight: bold;
}

table.moduletable {
        width: 100%;
        margin-bottom: 5px;
```

```
        padding: 0px;
        border-spacing: 0px;
        border-collapse: collapse;
}

div.moduletable {
    padding: 0;
    margin-bottom: 2px;
}

table.moduletable th, div.moduletable h3 {
    background: url(../images/subhead_bg.png) repeat-x;
    font-family: Trebuchet MS, Helvetica, Arial;
    color: #34300A;
    text-align: left;
    padding-left: 4px;
    height: 21px;
    line-height: 21px;
    font-weight: bold;
    font-size: 12px;
    text-transform: uppercase;
    margin: 0 0 2px 0;
}

table.moduletable td {
    font-size: 11px;
    padding: 0px;
    margin: 0px;
    font-weight: normal;
}

table.pollstableborder td {
  padding: 2px;
}

.sectiontableheader {
  font-weight: bold;
  background: #f0f0f0;
  padding: 4px;
}

.sectiontablefooter {

}
```

```
.sectiontableentry1 {
    background-color : #eee9db;
}

.sectiontableentry2 {
    background-color : #e3dabd;
}

.small {
    color: #999999;
    font-size: 11px;
}

.createdate {
    height: 15px;
    padding-bottom: 10px;
    color: #999999;
    font-size: 11px;
}

.modifydate {
    height: 15px;
    padding-top: 10px;
    color: #999999;
    font-size: 11px;
}

table.contenttoc {
  padding: 2px;
  margin-left: 2px;
  margin-bottom: 2px;
}

table.contenttoc td {
  padding: 2px;
}

table.contenttoc th {
  background: url(../images/subhead_bg.png) repeat-x;
  color: #666666;
    text-align: left;
    padding-top: 2px;
    padding-left: 4px;
    height: 21px;
```

```
        font-weight: bold;
        font-size: 10px;
        text-transform: uppercase;
}

a.mainlevel:link, a.mainlevel:visited {
        display: block;
        background: url(../images/menu_bg.png) no-repeat;
        vertical-align: middle;
        font-family: Trebuchet MS, Helvetica, Arial;
        font-size: 12px;
        font-weight: bold;
        color: #ccc;
        text-align: left;
        padding-top: 5px;
        padding-left: 18px;
        height: 20px !important;
        height: 25px;
        width: 100%;
        text-decoration: none;
}

a.mainlevel:hover {
        background-position: 0px -25px;
        text-decoration: none;
        color: #2C2014;
}

a.mainlevel#active_menu {
        color:#fff;
        font-weight: bold;
}

a.mainlevel#active_menu:hover {
        color: #fff;
}

a.sublevel:link, a.sublevel:visited {
        padding-left: 1px;
        vertical-align: middle;
        font-size: 11px;
        font-weight: bold;
        color: #c64934;
        text-align: left;
```

```
}

a.sublevel:hover {
    color: #900;
    text-decoration: none;
}

a.sublevel#active_menu {
    color: #333;
}

.highlight {
    background-color: Yellow;
    color: Blue;
    padding: 0;
}
.code {
    background-color: #ddd;
    border: 1px solid #bbb;
}

form {
/* removes space below form elements */
    margin: 0;
    padding: 0;
}

div.mosimage {
  border: 1px solid #ccc;
}

.mosimage {
  margin: 5px
}

.mosimage_caption {
  margin-top: 2px;
  background: #efefef;
  padding: 1px 2px;
  color: #666;
  font-size: 10px;
  border-top: 1px solid #cccccc;
}
```

```
span.article_seperator {
    display: block;
    height: 1.5em;
}
```

Table-Less Design

The second half of Chapter 3 covered creating a table-less, all CSS design from scratch using the same theme and images from the `rhuk_solarflare_ii` redesign. The final semantic, SEO-friendly, and user-friendly design looks like this:

Figure A.2: The final table-less design

The CSS

```
/* css */

/*////////// GENERAL //////////*/
    body {
```

```
    margin-top: 0px;
    margin-bottom: 30px;
      background-color: #070706;
      background-image: url("../images/main_bg.jpg");
      background-repeat: repeat-x;
      background-position: top left;
      background-attachment: fixed;
      font-family: "Trebuchet MS", Arial, Helvetica, sans-serif;
  }

#container {
  width: 850px;
  margin: 0 auto;
    margin-top: 20px;
  font-family: Verdana, Arial, Helvetica, sans-serif;
  font-size: 11px;
  color: #666666;
    background-color: #e3dabd;
  }

#container2 {
  width: 850px;
  margin: 0 auto;
  font-family: Verdana, Arial, Helvetica, sans-serif;
  font-size: 11px;
  line-height: 1.6em;
  color: #666666;
  }

#container3 {
  width: 635px;
    float: left;
  font-family: Verdana, Arial, Helvetica, sans-serif;
  font-size: 11px;
  line-height: 1.6em;
  color: #666666;
  }

h1 {
  font-weight: bold;
  font-size: 32px;
  color: #2c2014;
  margin-bottom: 30px;
  }
```

```css
h2 {
  font-weight: bold;
  color: #586230;
  font-size: 16px;
  }

h3 {
  font-weight: bold;
  font-size: 14px;
  color: #2c2014;
}

a {
  color: #2c2014;
  text-decoration: none;
  font-weight: bold;
  }

a:hover {
  color: #586230;
  font-weight: bold;
  text-decoration: underline;
  }

/*////////// HEADERS //////////*/
#header {
  width: 830px;
    height: 226px;
  border: 1px solid #ff6600;
  padding-bottom: 10px;
  padding-top: 10px;
  clear: both;
    background: url("../images/my_nature_header.jpg") no-repeat
                                              left top;
    border: 10px solid #e3dabd;
    border-bottom: none;
}

#header p, #header h1{
  display: none;
}

/*////////// CONTENT //////////*/
#content {
```

```
        width: 400px;
        padding-left: 10px;
        padding-right: 10px;
        padding-top: 10px;
          float: right;
    }

/*////////// NAV //////////*/

/*this is the top navtab layout*/

#top_navlist {
    position: absolute;
    padding0px;
    top: 30px;
    margin-left: 10px;
  width:830px;

}

#mainlevel-nav{
    padding: 0;
    margin: 0;
    background-color: #586230;
    background: url(../images/subhead_bg.png);
    color: #fff;
    float: left;
    width: 100%;
    font-family: Trebuchet MS, Helvetica, Arial;
    font-weight: bold;
    font-size: 14px;
  line-height: 21px;
    border-bottom: 5px solid #e3dabd;
}

#mainlevel-nav li { display: inline; }

#mainlevel-nav li a {
    padding: 0.2em 1em;
  background-color: #586230;
    background: url(../images/subhead_bg.png);
    color: #e3dabd;
    text-decoration: none;
    float: left;
```

```
        border-right: 1px solid #e3dabd;
}
#mainlevel-nav li a:hover{
    background-color: #9f9882;
    background-image: none;
    color: #fff;
}

/*this is the main menu*/
#mainlevel {
    margin-left: 0;
    padding-left: 0;
    padding-top: 0px !important;
    padding-top: 10px;
    list-style-type: none;
}

#mainlevel a{
    display: block;
    padding: 3px;
    width: 180px;
    background-color: #343330;
    background-image: url("../images/menu_bg.png");
    border-bottom: 2px solid #e3dabd;
}

#mainlevel a#active_menu {
    background-position: 0px -25px;
    color: #FFF;
}

#mainlevel a:link, #mainlevel a:visited{
    color: #b7b092;
    text-decoration: none;
}

#mainlevel a:hover{
    background-color: #ada692;
    background-position: 0px -25px;
    color: #090806;
}
/*////////// RIGHT SIDEBAR //////////*/
    #sidebarRT {
        float: right;
```

```
        width: 185px;
        padding-left: 5px;
        padding-right: 10px;
        padding-top: 0px;
    }

/*////////// LEFT SIDEBAR //////////*/
    #sidebarLT {
        float: left;
        width: 180px;
        padding-left: 10px;
        padding-right: 10px;
        padding-top: 10px;
 }

 /*//////////Joomla Classes////////////*/
table.moduletable th, div.moduletable h3{
    background: url(../images/subhead_bg.png) repeat-x;
    font-family: Trebuchet MS, Helvetica, Arial;
    color: #34300A;
    text-align: left;
    padding-left: 4px;
    height: 21px;
    line-height: 21px;
    font-weight: bold;
    font-size: 12px;
    text-transform: uppercase;
    margin: 0 0 2px 0;
}

.contentheading {
    height: 30px;
    font-family: Trebuchet MS, Helvetica, Arial;
    color: #586230;
    font-weight: bold;
    font-size: 20px;
    white-space: nowrap;
}

span.article_seperator {
    display: block;
    height: 1.5em;
}
```

```
.back_button {
    float: left;
  text-align: center;
  font-size: 11px;
  font-weight: bold;
  border: 3px double #586230;
  width: auto;
  background: url(../images/button_bg.png) repeat-x;
  padding: 0px 10px;
  line-height: 20px;
  margin: 1px;
}

.pagenav {
  text-align: center;
  font-size: 11px;
  font-weight: bold;
  border: 3px double #586230;
  width: auto;
  background: url(../images/button_bg.png) repeat-x;
  padding: 0px 10px;
  line-height: 20px;
  margin: 1px;
}

/*////////// FORMS //////////*/
    .search {
     float: right;
     margin-top: -29px !important;
    margin-top: -49px;
     margin-right: .5em;
     color: #000;
    }

.inputbox {
    padding: 2px;
    border:solid 1px #34300A;
    background-color: #e3dabd;
    color: #000;
}

.button {
  color: #586230;
  font-family: Arial, Hevlvetica, sans-serif;
```

```
    text-align: center;
    font-size: 11px;
    font-weight: bold;
    border: 3px double #586230;
    width: auto;
    background: url(../images/button_bg.png) repeat-x;
    padding: 0px 5px;
    line-height: 18px !important;
    line-height: 16px;
    height: 26px !important;
    height: 24px;
    margin: 1px;
}


/*////////// FOOTER //////////*/
    #footer {
      margin-top: 15px;
      padding-top: 5px;
      padding-bottom:5px;
      clear: both;
      width: 830px;
      background-color:#070706;
        border: 10px solid #e3dabd;
        color: #FFF;
    }

    #footer p {
      color:#FFFFFF;
      padding: 5px;
      text-align: center;
    }

    #footer a {
      color: #766b33;
      font-weight:bold;
  }

    #footer a:hover {
      color: #FFFFFF;
      text-decoration: none;
      border-bottom: 1px solid #FFF;
  }
```

The XHTML and PHP

```php
<?php defined( '_VALID_MOS' ) or die( 'Direct Access to this location
                                    is not allowed.' ); ?>
<!DOCTYPE html PUBLIC "-//W3C//DTD XHTML 1.0 Transitional//EN"
                             "http://www.w3.org/TR/xhtml1/DTD/
                             xhtml1-transitional.dtd">
<html xmlns="http://www.w3.org/1999/xhtml"
                            lang="<?php echo _LANGUAGE; ?>"
                            xml:lang="<?php echo _LANGUAGE; ?>">
<head>
<meta http-equiv="Content-Type" content="text/html;
                                    <?php echo _ISO; ?>" />
<?php
if ($my->id) { initEditor(); } ?>
<?php mosShowHead(); ?>

<script type="text/javascript"> </script>
<style type="text/css" media="screen">

    @import url("<?php echo $mosConfig_live_site;?>/templates/
                      my_NEW_nature_design/css/template_css.css");

</style>

</head>
<body>
<!--<a name="top"></a>-->
<div id="container"><!--container goes here-->

<div id="header">

<h1><?php echo $mosConfig_sitename; ?></h1>
</div><!--//header-->

<!-- Begin #container2 this holds the content and sidebars-->
<div id="container2">

<!-- Begin #container3 keeps the left col and body positioned-->
<div id="container3">
<!-- Begin #content -->
<div id="content">
<?php mospathway() ?>
<?php mosMainBody(); ?>
</div><!-- //content -->

<!-- #left sidebar -->
<div id="sidebarLT">
```

```
<?php mosLoadModules('left', -2);?>
<?php mosLoadModules('right', -2);?>


</div><!--//sidebarLT  -->
</div><!--//container3-->

<!-- #right sidebar -->
<div id="sidebarRT">
<?php mosLoadModules('top', -2);?>
<?php mosLoadModules('user1', -2);?>
<?php mosLoadModules('user2', -2);?>


</div><!--//sidebarRT -->


<!--<div id="falseBottm">
</div>--><!--//falseBottm-->

</div><!--//container2-->


<!--<a name="mainNav"> </a>-->
<div id="tabbar"> </div>

<div id="top_navlist">
<?php mosLoadModules ( 'user3', -2 ); ?>
<?php mosLoadModules ( 'user4', -2 ); ?>

</div>
<!--//top_navlist-->


<div id="footer">
<?php include_once($mosConfig_absolute_path.'/includes/
                                          footer.php');?>


</div><!--//footer-->

</div><!--//container-->

</body>
</html>
```

Index

Symbols

A

C

D

E

F

G

container divs 90
CSS trouble-shooting technique 91

P

Pizazzz 127
Prototype 157

R

Rhuk Redesign
  CSS code 188-201
  CSS code, table-less design 202-209
  XHTML and PHP code, table-less design
    210, 211
RIA 147
Rich Interface Applications 147
rounded corners
  four corners 164, 165
  module, customizing 169, 170
  two image cheat 167, 168
  two images, using 165-167

S

Script.alico.us 157
Search Engine Optimization. *See* SEO
semantic
  about 60
  structure 67
SEO
  about 180
  descriptions 182
  keywords 181, 182
  URLs 180, 181
servers 30
sizable text
  about 170
  em sizing 171
SmoothGallery 160
Strict DOCTYPE 63
Suckerfish method 129
SuckeroomlaFish
  CSS, applying to Joomla! 132-134
  DOM script, applying to Joomla! 135
  extend menu module, installing 131, 132

T

table-less design 202
tables
  mainBody();, customizing 184
  removing 182-185
template, designing
  about 5
  color scheme, defining 20
  CSS, prerequisites 9
  Flash 136
  icons, choosing 24
  Joomla!, prerequisites 7
  key elements, identifying 11
  prerequisites 7
  tips 163
  versus web page designing 6
  XHTML, prerequisites 8
  XML 100
templates
  AJAX, implementing 149
  built-in 12
  colors, changing 50-54
  content, adding 73-75
  creating 37-40
  designing tips 163
  DOCTYPE 63
  images, adding 55-59
  images, changing 55-59
  Joomla!, uploading to 110
  layout 66-71
  main body 65
  making changes 41-49
  module options 76, 77
  modules, adding 72-75
  packaging 109, 110
  styling 78, 79
  thumbnail, creating 99
thumbnail
  creating 99
Transitional DOCTYPE 63
troubleshooting
  about 83
  advanced 86
  basics 83-86
  casing 84

V

validation
about 92-94
advanced 96
Firebug 97
Firefox's JavaScript/error console 96, 97

W

web page designing
versus template designing 6
web servers 30
workflow
Firefox 36
setting up 35
template, adding images 55-59
template, changing images 55-59

template, creating 37-40
template, making changes 41-49
template color, changing 50-54
Wrapper Menu Item
about 153
uses 153
using 154-156
WYSIWYG editors
about 31, 178
disadvantages 31

X

XHTML
semantic 60
XML document
template, designing 100-108

Building Websites with Joomla! 1.5 Beta 1

ISBN: 978-1-847192-38-7   Paperback: 380 pages

The bestselling Joomla tutorial guide updated for the latest download release

1. Install and configure Joomla! 1.5 beta 1

2. Customize and extend your Joomla! site

3. Create your own template and extensions

4. **Free eBook upgrades up to 1.5 Final Release**

5. Also available covering Joomla v1

Learning Joomla! Extension Development

ISBN: 978-1-847191-30-4   Paperback: 200 pages

A practical tutorial for creating your first Joomla! 1.5 extensions with PHP

1. Program your own extensions to Joomla!

2. Create new, self-contained components with both back-end and front-end functionality

3. Create configurable site modules to show information on every page

4. Distribute your extensions to other Joomla! users

Please check **www.PacktPub.com** for information on our titles

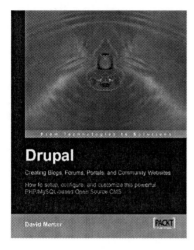

Drupal

ISBN: 1-904811-80-9 Paperback: 267 pages

How to setup, configure and customise this powerful PHP/MySQL based Open Source CMS

1. Install, configure, administer, maintain and extend Drupal

2. Control access with users, roles and permissions

3. Structure your content using Drupal's powerful CMS features

4. Includes coverage of release 4.7

Learning Mambo

ISBN: 1-904811-62-0 Paperback: 300 pages

A well-structured and example-rich tutorial to creating websites using Mambo

1. A practical step-by-step tutorial to creating your Mambo website

2. Master all the important aspects of Mambo, including menus, content management, and templates

3. Gain hands-on experience by developing an example site through the book

Please check **www.PacktPub.com** for information on our titles

Printed in the United States
101160LV00005B/40/A